AF472411

# The Last National Service Man

# The Last National Service Man

Conrad Bryant

Copyright 2009 Conrad Bryant

ISBN 978-1-4452-5304-6

# Contents

# Foreword

National service was not voluntary for men in the UK when I was younger. All men over eighteen who were medically fit and not in a restricted occupation, coal mining was one for instance, were "called up" as it was termed for two years. In earlier years the call up came at age eighteen, but as national service was run down and fewer men were needed, your call up papers came later. I was nineteen when mine came.

You had no choice about going or not, unless you liked prison that is. Similarly you had no choice of which service you went into either, or so it appeared to me. I cannot for instance think why I would have chosen the RAF. No relative of mine had served in the RAF, and I had never been in an aeroplane.

I actually started my national service on the second of December 1958. Fifty-two days later I deserted to the ranks of the regulars due to the terribly poor pay of the national service man, plus the unlikely possibility of being posted overseas. I signed on for three years and actually finished my service in January 1962. I kept my national service number, my uniform and my outlook on the service however, right up until my demob in 1962.

So on the second of December I became 5065237 A.C. U.T. Bryant. Or Bryant 237 for short. I was no longer a person with a first name or even the title Mr. Incidentally I do not know if they thought Army men were cleverer than RAF men but they were called by their surname followed by four numbers. They must have thought that the RAF men would have got tired remembering four numbers not three.

While technically I suppose I was not actually the very last national service man called up, I was in one of the last batches, as I know of men just a few months younger than I was, who were medically fit, yet never received the call. The following is a personal view of my service looked at from a non-military viewpoint. I hope you enjoy it.

Bryant 237.

# Chapter One

## 1958 The Beginning

In 1958 I became one of the last of a rapidly dying breed, The National service Man. These men were called upon to live and act constantly on the knife-edge of military campaigns and operations, or that's my story after a few pints. Without these willing, battle hardened, determined, courageous and dedicated troops it is difficult to understand how the RAF (pronounced raaf) pay accounts could have survived. These true (well only slightly embellished) stories are dedicated to this band of fearless modern day warriors of their time.

It is only right that I should now declare that I would not have missed it for the world. While some will argue that for many individuals, and indeed the government's financial and operational needs, national service towards the end of its life was an absolute waste, for me it was an experience not to be missed.

Again it is only right that at this point I declare my defection to the ranks of the (thick) regulars after only 52 days service as a national service man, although for the next three years I managed to play the double role of "thick regular" and "clever national service man" as it suited me. I retained by stealth my national service uniform, poor though it was compared to the regulars, my number and outlook. The reasons for my defection were simple. Money and a chance of a free overseas holiday. National service pay was a joke. A "poor" joke in more ways than one, but nevertheless a joke. Secondly I was told that national service men were no longer to be posted overseas. This I found out later to be untrue but at the time appeared correct. After basic and trade training, despite volunteering for Christmas Island, I was eventually given an overseas posting, for a Welsh man at least, Weston Super

Mare. Not what I had hoped for, but who got what they wanted in the RAF? Weston Super Mare's weather to be kind could be said to be not as nice as Christmas Island, though I later found out that the nuclear radiation level was lower. My idea of going overseas meant crossing a larger expanse of water than was necessary to cross from Cardiff to Weston. Pity about the sea at Weston never coming in to meet the beach, I could probably have seen it just as well from Christmas Island. Still more about Weston later.

As a regular I eventually got my overseas posting to Kenya via Aden. Those two years in Kenya more than made up for any loses in other spheres of life. I still have strikingly vivid memories of the awesome Victoria Falls, majestic wild animals, being thrown out of a game park, playing sports I had not heard of before, trying to win the "make the officer salute you first" competition, and hitch hiking hundreds of miles just for a sandwich and the devilment, but they are stories for later and I should get back to the beginning.

The true beginning was the letter telling me to report to a building in Newport for my medical examination. So on the appointed day a few of us from my village set off for Newport. I think the doctor was the most unfit person I had seen to date. Fat red faced and smoking. Now the medical was not exactly rigorous. You stood outside a door and knocked. A distant voice shouted, "come in". You opened the door and walked in. By now you were half way through the medical, having passed the hearing test, you had heard his call; the intelligence test, unaided you had understood the command and opened the door; and the physical test, you had walked in. All that was left was to cough, so that the doctor could warm his hands on your lower regions, and confirm that you had no serious illness. I had a tougher medical to get a job as a clerk with the National Coal Board, but they were a tougher organisation I suppose.

I vividly remember arriving at my first camp, RAF Cardington, confused and feeling lost. I tramped through this huge hall along with other lost souls being given things and clothes seemingly at random. I had never seen a button stick before and could not guess what its use was. Was it some modern weapon for use in case of a nuclear attack? No. It turned out to be a device you slid behind your brass buttons so that when you cleaned them the material of your uniform did not get marked. Clever these RAF scientists. I was given a set of "irons".

A knife, a fork and a spoon. The spoon's main purpose was to do with your boots, not eating as you would think, but I will return to that in a moment. The only item of clothing that size seemed to matter slightly were your shoes and boots. Incidentally with the boots did anyone discover why they came with pimples on the toe caps, which you then had to burn off with the handle of a spoon, heated over a candle after dark, so that the toe caps were smooth. Such a discovery led me to believe that I truly had entered a mad house, and till the end of my service I constantly confused the brush to put the shoe polish on with the one to brush it off. But did it matter? Incidentally I still have my shoe brushes but have lost my button stick.

Now the national service uniform was a sight to behold. Elegant it was not. Comfortable it was not. Warm, OK it was warm. In the winter this was good but can anyone remember how stupid we looked in the summer. Shirtsleeves rolled up with a tie I suppose was reasonable, but the national service trousers with no jacket was a real joke. They were designed to be worn with braces, again OK with a coat on. But with no coat on and held up by the belt from your jacket while still having the high cut peaks in the back for the braces showing made us look like cartoon characters. That they were all very baggy added to the comic character illusion. We all seemed to have high waists and stomachs and short chests. The only saving grace was that all of us looked stupid. It got worse however when we eventually mixed in with the regulars. They had short jackets and their trousers were cut like normal trousers with a regular straight waist, but again I get ahead of myself.

# Chapter Two

## Training

Once we were kited out it was off to our new holiday camp. Square bashing! RAF Bridgenorth. Eight weeks of marching, rifle drill and toilet cleaning. My intake was lucky in some respect in that Christmas fell during our eight weeks so we had a break. What are my most vivid memories of those weeks? The first that springs to mind is clearing ice and snow from the roads around our billet with a piece of stick about a foot long and about an inch thick. I cannot remember now if this was a punishment or were we taking the Mickey out of our NCO's. To be fair to our drill instructors (and that is hard to do) they were probably not selected for their mastermind qualities, but I suppose for their loud voices and ability to not go mad with our efforts at marching and rifle drill. The only sharp thing about them were the slashed peaks on their peaked caps. And talking of marching, can you remember the few recruits who just had to march putting both right arm and right leg forward at the same time instead of alternatively. Even the rest of us laughed at them, but they were a disaster to march behind.

For eight weeks we marched, marched and marched again. Again to be fair to our drill instructors they did get us to march well and all together by the end of the eight weeks. I think that by the end of our training we almost enjoyed hearing the rhythmic crunch of our studded boots on the tarmac. Perhaps I am getting a little carried away with it now as it was a long time ago and I cannot recall rushing into our hut at night excited at how well we had marched that day.

Incidentally the training must have been thorough and really drummed into us though as I can still do the rifle drill movements now some forty years later, although it has to be said I do not find a great deal of use for this skill.

I have a photograph of Hut 260, RAF Bridgenorth, and a gormless lot we look too. There are many angles you can wear a RAF peaked cap at other than square on your head as it is supposed to be worn, and in the photo our squad has obviously mastered all of them. Thinking about it, it is no wonder that our drill instructors always seemed annoyed and uptight. When we progressed to rifle drill the instructors expected a good hard crack from the rifle when you hit it with your hand at the end of or during a movement. Now there was a hard and an easy way to achieve a louder noise. Hit the rifle harder with your hand, or loosen the screws slightly on the rifle so it rattled more when stuck. Most opted as you would expect for the second option. We never fired these rifles, and had to remember to tighten the screws again before rifle inspection, but it worked well.

Another vivid memory of RAF Bridgenorth is language. Rather I suppose I mean the number of English languages there are, or so it appeared. I thought that I spoke English even though I came from Wales, but if that was the case what were the other recruits speaking as I could not understand them speaking, yet most of them came from England. Now, of course, the culture shock would not be so great as we all hear different dialects and accents on television. In those days there was no mass television viewing and foreign holidays for me meant a day visit to Bristol Zoo. The first few days I just could not understand what the others were saying. Likewise they could not understand me. Then after a week a change took place. Every time I spoke a strange voice was heard. It appeared my voice had changed or that someone else was speaking for me. It was of course my hearing adjusting, but I could still not understand the others. Then a full transformation took place. My seemingly strange voice disappeared and I could understand the others, well all bar the Scots and the Geordies, though that came eventually. Even in later years when I had good friends who were Scots and Geordies I could not understand them when they got excited.

I cannot remember anything personal about the men in my group, as I never seemed to get very friendly with anyone. Possibly it was because I could not understand what they were saying? Looking back through my photographs I do see that AC Denman was the only man who I was with at my first camp for kitting out, was with me at square bashing, hut 260, and was also on the same course as I was for pay accounts training at RAF Hereford. I never saw him again, nor any of the other people I trained with but that is what it is like in the RAF.

RAF shirts had detached collars attached by two studs. To save time in the morning we soon discovered that if you undid the front stud only plus a few buttons and then loosened your tie you could take off your shirt, collar and tie as one unit. In the morning the reverse took only a few moments for you to be half dressed again.

The system made you childish though. I remember that after six weeks we were allowed to wear our bayonet in its scabbard while doing drill. We all felt superior at this and seemed to look down on those recruits a few weeks behind us, who did not have this apparent honour. How simple we had become!

The weather was bitterly cold with snow on the ground. We seemed to march all day and bull up our kit and our hut all evening. The regular hut and kit inspections were supposed to teach us order and discipline but I am not sure if they succeeded or not. Some mornings we were expected to have our kit gleaming ready for inspection after being out on guard duty all night. To have gleaming polished boots ready for inspection after wearing them out in the snow all night was an impossibility, but we were supposed to. Remember National Service Men only had one pair of boots.

An interesting exercise was trying to have a dust free hut when the form of heating was two old coal fired stoves in the middle of the room. Still there were 20 of us in the hut to do it all. I well remember that we were expected to make up our bed with the blankets stretched so tight that a coin dropped in the centre of the bed from less than shoulder height was expected to bounce.

Another interesting thing was firing real bullets, or live rounds as the instructors liked to call it. I had never fired a gun of any description before and always wondered after my firing range performance how they ever let me near a gun again. I was a terrible shot but I think the instructors must have been set certain targets they had to achieve in getting us to shoot straight. Nothing else can explain how I came to be classed as a first class shot. I did not reach marksman level as not even our instructors could get it that wrong.

Bayonet training was another joy. We were required to run towards a sack of sand suspended from a scaffold and stab it in the middle, twist the bayonet to loosen it and presumably cause more internal damage to our victim, then withdraw it and run to the next target. I still recall that when we had to stab a marker on the ground, a supposed enemy on the floor, many missed. The sarcastic NCO standing there took great delight in reminding those who missed that they were now dead.

Now quick thinking can get you out of a lot of trouble as I often found out in my time in the RAF. I recall on the firing range calling the grumpy Welsh Sergeant "Taff". He heard me and exploded at the familiarity demanding to know what right I had to be familiar with him. My quick reply was that I had not called him "Taff" but "staff". Staff being an abbreviated form of address for a staff sergeant, a higher rank than a sergeant. This swift apparent promotion soothed him immediately and I got away with it. Not the last time quick thinking helped me in my three years in the RAF.

Next came trade training. RAF Hereford, Number Two School of Admin Trades. As usual with the RAF it did not go as planned. The RAF system is not like the army where people move as a block. We all made our own way to our next camp after a few days leave. They just gave us a rail pass and expected us to get on with it and get to our destination on time. To be fair it worked as well. When I arrived the course I was to be on was cancelled or delayed or something so in true Monty Python style I was allocated, temporarily, to the pay accounts course. Apparently they forgot it was a temporary transfer and pay accounts I was for my three years. I cannot remember much about this course except that as I had worked in a real office for two years it was too simple for words. My photograph states that the course lasted from 12$^{th}$ February to 25$^{th}$ March 1959. My body language in the photo suggests I was fed up with the course, as I am the only one with folded arms and a grim expression. Still I passed.

# Chapter Three

## Weston Super Mare

My first real posting to a RAF camp was RAF Locking in Weston Super Mare. It was 1959 and I was a pay clerk on apprentice's pay. Real front line shock troop. Here I should make an apology to Apprentice Smythe. My ledger was apprentices S to Z. I therefore had all the Smiths. I think there were about 20 of them plus my one Smythe. I wonder is he reading this. If he is I hope he can now laugh at it. As pay clerk, one of my duties every week was to call out the names of the apprentices on my pay roll and tell the officer how much to pay them. Every week I called out Smith 20 times, and disciplined as they were, they each came forward in the correct order, gave their number, saluted and collected their pay. When Smythe's turn came up I called out Smith, as Smythe to me at that time was too posh a name for anyone. No reply. We moved on. At the end of the pay parade there alone stood a solitary apprentice. Smythe. He of course got paid, but usually last. I did not do it every parade but quite often. Congratulations to him though he would not give in to me and my little game, though I bet he celebrated when I was posted away.

Life in pay accounts in Weston was not exactly strenuous. In fact the most difficult thing was trying to look reasonably busy when you had nothing at all to do. There were four of us doing what was really an easy job for one, but that was RAF life for you. Time passed, but slowly, and was only bearable due to the games you were able to play on other people. Childish games they appear now, but to a bored 19 year old they did not seem that way then.

My favourite game again involved the pay parade. The system officially was that we calculated the pay for all apprentices on our ledger, totalled up the cash requirement and "coined up". This involved calculating how many pound notes, half crowns, sixpences etc were needed to pay everyone out the correct sum. This was passed to an officer who collected the cash. On the pay parade I would call out the name of the apprentice, he would answer by replying "Sir" followed by the last three numbers of his service number. I then called out the amount to be paid from my ledger and the officer sitting on my left checked this as I entered it in the paid column. The senior officer then placed the correct sum of money in front of the apprentice from the piles in front of him, this being sight checked by the officer sitting on his right hand side. A foolproof system. At least it was if everything went correctly.

Unfortunately for some of the officers they seemed to think that erks like me who were in the ranks were not fully paid up members of the human race. When they were often no older than you, with no longer service than you, clearly no brighter than you, but felt superior, for example insisting on being saluted when you first met them, again on leaving, with constantly expecting the word "sir" to be used at least once in each sentence, they were really asking for trouble, and of course we could give it to them. You must remember that we were daily working with numbers while they only attended irregularly. The favourite trick was to coin up using a different formula to the normally accepted one. For example seven shillings and sixpence in old money could be made up of three half crowns or three two shilling pieces plus a shilling plus a sixpence. By not using the normal method of "coining up" and letting the officer pay out in the accepted method, it meant that towards the end of the pay parade, the coins left would not make up the correct amounts to be paid out. Thereupon the three officers ended up searching through their pockets for change. Of course you sat there looking innocent, as it was obviously their mistake somewhere, which they believed. Newer officers especially could become quite flustered much to the enjoyment of myself and any apprentices remaining. Childish as I said but satisfying revenge. Life during the day was not exciting.

The other game was to gradually speed up during the pay parade, which again could make the officers confused. They would not wish to lose face by asking you to slow down, and of course if they did you went very slow. Not good for their image and remember they were mostly young too.

Our billets at Locking were the best I ever had. Four to a room, not 22. Real luxury. Relative privacy. Polished oilcloth floor, big windows, plastered not wooden walls, ample fitted lockers and lights and bookrack above your bed. I was lucky and had good roommates all the time I was there. I cannot remember the names of any of them now but one came from the Wells area of Somerset and went home every weekend I seem to remember. My main friend I suppose was Brian. Brian Bodfish a Brummie. He was not in my room but we were together on most things while I was stationed in Weston. One time he visited my home and I showed him a Rhondda night out. Another weekend I visited his home and we spent the night out in Birmingham. I still remember at the end of that night in the Bullring burning my lip on a Fleur de lis pie. Hope the spelling is right. Brian played centre forward and was noted for being able to get the ball in the net if it was given to him close to goal. In those days I believe forwards could be a little more robust with goalkeepers!

The thing that sticks mainly in my mind about our billets was that we all walked around our room on thick blanket material type pads just larger than our shoes. At first it seemed madness but actually it was a good idea. It meant that we never scratched or dirtied the floor, and it was constantly being buffed up so always retained its shine. Saved a lot of "bulling up" come the infrequent inspections.

The food at Locking was the usual RAF food. If you were young and we all were, hungry and with cast iron constitutions it was good. It was in the RAF that I learned eating manners and systems that were new to me. Firstly speed was essential unless you liked cold food. Secondly breakfast was always eaten cooked food first followed by cereals. Simple really, your cereals were supposed to be cold and so could wait to be eaten, although the cornflakes could get soggy if you ate your cooked breakfast slowly, hence the haste. The option of queuing for each course separately and eating that course before queuing again was not an option really. Took too long. The best food I ever came across was my first year in Kenya before the audit of food costs took place, but that is another story later.

The social life outside of camp varied. Your friends were fine, the beer was good, red barrel was the in drink at the time, the females were a little scarce on the ground however especially if you were so obviously RAF. With my accent there was no way I could pass as a local. A few of us found a way around this to a certain extent by taking dance lessons. The females there had to dance with you, as that is what they were there for as well. At least you got close enough to put an arm around one and try to chat them up. Did not always work but it was more successful than any other method I found there. It was there that I learned to dance. Well that's a slight exaggeration. It was there that I learned to do a quick step to all dance music other then the Cha Cha. The late night walks back to the camp, alone if you had been successful earlier, took a while but we were young and could take the late nights and lack of sleep.

Talking of red barrel, and the thought of drinking a gallon of it now makes me feel weak, reminds me of our Wednesday nights out. At six o clock precisely the door of our regular pub opened and we filed in. Sitting on the bar were three pints of red barrel. If the irregular fourth member of our party was there another pint followed in swift time. After a serious tasting session of the beer our darts practice started, and did we need the practice. After sampling, for medicinal purposes only of course, three or four pints, it was time to go around the town for a drink or the pictures. Weston was not the most vibrant town especially on a Wednesday night. Looking back we were really stuck in a rut weren't we.

My journey back and forth from Cardiff to Weston on the weekends I went home were by paddle steamer. From home it meant two bus journeys plus a ride on a tram, then by the paddle steamer across the Bristol Channel. It was an exhilarating voyage during the winter at night with the spray flying everywhere and the paddle wheels churning away steadily. Fascinating to watch the pistons driving the wheels from inside while watching the awesome power of the sea outside on wilder nights. They no longer run of course but so much has changed.

At Weston we landed at the multi level landing stage depending on the state of the tide. The walk to the town was quite a step if you had things to carry. Buses cost money and while I suppose there were taxis I never gave them a thought. They would have been a waste of good beer money if there were any anyway. While it was relatively easy to travel home for weekends I did not go home often as this was my first real taste of life away from home and so had to be enjoyed.

Life at RAF Locking was too quiet for me and I had a permanent application in for an overseas posting, and soon things were going to take a dramatic turn for the better.

# Chapter Four

## Overseas At Last To Aden

At last my real overseas posting came through. Aden! Well sunnier than Weston I had to agree. Then came more news. I was entitled to many weeks embarkation leave and while no one had told me, I was entitled to many more weeks extra leave because I had signed on for the extra year. To say personnel matters in the RAF were slow is to put it mildly. At first it seemed that I would not have time to take all my leave and still go abroad before my three years were up, but it was not quite like that.

So home to Gilfach Goch in the Rhondda for a few months.

Now while on this holiday from RAF Locking I think I created a first in RAF history. It was customary for airmen to be given a forty eight-hour pass, which meant you were free for two days. Many who lived near enough went home. Nobody who was off camp for an extended period ever came back to camp for those forty-eight hours. I did. It occurred when I was home on embarkation leave prior to leaving for Aden. I had nine weeks leave. Anyway while on this leave a few of my friends on camp were leaving so I had to go back to be at their demob party didn't I. I actually spent nearly a whole week back there so I suppose the food and beer could not have been too bad. My diary records that I spent our usual Wednesday night out down the Elm Tree having a few pints and playing darts with Brian and Ken Cornaly, hope the spelling is right as my handwriting is not the best.

Looking at my diary it seems hard to believe that in those nine weeks at home I did not drown in beer. It records that one night Graham Oatley, my closest friend, and Bruice Hughes and I travelled back from a night out on the back of a beer lorry to Bruice's house. In exchange for free accommodation we drank the complimentary small barrel of beer the driver was allowed, or so he told us.

During this period Graham went back to his posting in Germany with me accompanying him to Cardiff to see him off and of course help out the Cardiff landlords.

During this period of extended leave my diary records that I was doing very well in "pulling the birds" as we used to call it. It also records that I never went out with one more than once or twice. Either I chose them badly in the first place or they quickly got fed up with me. Don't think I'll try to find out now, as it might not be good news even if they could remember me.

As I have said before RAF personnel moving station is very much an individual operation. On the appointed day however I duly arrived at Innesworth. My papers were in order and after being kitted out with tropical clothes, and hanging around for two weeks, I was packed onto a plane at RAF Hendon for Aden. I flew in a Britannia aircraft and the fight took eleven hours. Seems impossible but that is what I have recorded. Perhaps we landed somewhere? Temperature ninety in the shade.

So this new, by now well trained pay clerk, arrives and surprise, surprise they did not need another body in pay accounts. With typical RAF efficiency the game of pass the parcel commences. Muggins here being the parcel. It must be admitted that I was a very relaxed parcel. My sole duty while I waited to hear my fate appeared to be to go to the mess at meal times, and that was not obligatory, gentle sunbathing by day, a little sight seeing, and by night a few quiet pints. O yes I was required to do some fatigues when they remembered I was there but they were not stressful. It always was a tough life in the RAF but this was really bearable. The accommodation was interesting. Large barrack blocks with high large doors and wide verandas on which were beds. I slept out under the stars but on the first morning realised why I got that prime bed space so easily. I was on the wrong side of the building and the sun woke me up very early. Much too early especially as I had nothing to do all day.

My first recollection that first day as anyone who has been stationed in Khormaksar will remember was the echoing call around the area of "mooneeeeee !!!" when a white skinned body like me appeared. They were all brown of course and I had just come from the UK in

March and was on the pale side. I resolved straight away to change that as quickly as possible without going bright red. Luckily I am dark skinned and it did not take long. Certainly by the time I got to Kenya two weeks later I was a suitably camouflaged brown.

I stayed in Aden for two weeks. Apparently I would have got a medal of some sort if I had been on the permanent staff but did not qualify as I was in transit. I would have thought that a stray bullet would have been as painful for me as someone on the permanent staff, but there you go. I was not much of a one for medals anyway. So I had two weeks in Aden exploring beaches and the town. Many areas were out of bounds and being new to foreign countries I obeyed the rules and stayed in the permitted areas. Certainly different and exciting is the best way to describe Aden at that time. Plus of course hot. One beach there seemed to go on forever and mirages were an almost permanent feature. Aden had its contrasts however. I still have a photograph of a dwelling of a poor person, which is just two loosely built stone walls about three feet high around the mouth of a cave and covered by a few loose corrugated sheets. Yet in the town some of the shops stocked the most expensive cameras and watches you could imagine.

Haggling in the shops was compulsory I had been warned. I still remember buying my first camera there, a Braun, and taking at least half an hour to negotiate the price down. I am sure he still made a handsome profit. Outside the shop I thought why not buy a light meter as well as I had paid less than I thought I would have to for the camera. Back in I go. Patter all ready for a long session. He gave me one look asked what I wanted stated his price and when I started my spiel he just looked at me shrugged and made it clear he had had enough bargaining with me and that was his bottom price. I got a bargain but felt slightly cheated out of the entertainment.

Young boys were everywhere offering watches or their sister for sale. There were no buyers in my group. Anyway we all had watches.

Our uniform had now changed of course. Too hot for RAF Blue. We all dressed the same now, both National Service Men and Regulars. Khaki shirt with the sleeves rolled up, long shorts, soon to be shortened, long socks up to the knee and black shoes. Plus of course blue berets. I liked this uniform as it was practical and comfortable. Our "best" uniform I was not so keen on but we very rarely used it. It was a simple change from Khaki shorts to longs worn with a full length bush type jacket.

In my days the big birthday was your twenty first. Now most people had a party for their twenty first birthday. It is usually a well planned affair with friends and family invited. Food and drinks laid on. Perhaps music and some dancing. Well not for me. I forgot about my twenty first birthday until about ten thirty that night. I remembered as I was filling out the pre flight forms to fly from Aden to Kenya. When I had left the UK it was about two weeks before my birthday and I had assumed I would be well settled in Aden by the big day. Little did I realise that I would only be in transit there. With no job to do the time gets jumbled up. So I missed it. By the time we landed in Kenya the day had gone so it was best forgotten, it is just another day after all.

So no birthday party for me on my twenty first. I looked on my posting to Kenya as probably one of the best birthday presents I could have had though. I celebrated without telling anyone on the plane by drinking a cup of in flight RAF tea. Ugh.

Aden was the only place where it was necessary to take salt tablets to combat the loss of salts through sweating. The first few days I didn't take them although they were on the tables in the mess at every meal. I soon felt the effect. You soon have a pain in the stomach and feel weak and sick. A couple of tablets and you are back to normal.

For some strange reason I liked Aden. I think most people thought me mad but soon I was on my way to Kenya. Would they be expecting me there I thought. Well yes and no. They had heard a national service man was coming to pay accounts but they had no real vacancy, but that never caused a problem in the RAF

# Chapter Five

## RAF Eastleigh, Kenya

I spent two years in Kenya. Two amazing wonderful years. My decision to desert the national service mans ranks and join the thick regulars was fully justified. As I was now myself a regular perhaps I should stop using the "thick regular" phrase, or perhaps not. The weather, the scenery, the wild animals and the people were all wonderful. So wonderful I almost signed on for more years, but as I could only spend less than another year in Kenya and the rest of the time in the UK I did not do it. So many good things happened to me that as I sit here now I feel that I should be employed by the Kenya tourist board as I am that excited just remembering those things and looking at my old photographs. I know that they say you only remember the good things and forget the bad, but in Kenya's case that rule does not apply, at least for me and my two years there. I still feel the attachment to Kenya, so much that whenever a Kenyan athlete or team competes in any sport I automatically support them, unless they are competing against Wales of course.

Let's start with the tale of the mess food to which I referred before. After over a year of RAF food the meals there were a revelation. At every meal the choice was great, the helpings large, the quality first class and the preparation good. There was more time to eat and the queues were less so sometimes you even went up separately to collect each course. Why was this I thought? Well after about a year reality hit us hard. The cookhouse had overspent their budget and cut backs were made. We were really brought back down to earth. While we still had the volume and no doubt it was still well prepared the choice and variety had gone forever. Still you can't win them all.

So what about what I laughingly called my work in the RAF in Kenya. I was still in pay accounts but now I was the sole clerk on civilian pay. As the Flight Sergeant in charge of accounts cannot touch me now I can admit that to put it mildly I was not stretched work wise, unless you consider working about three days a month at a relaxed pace being stretched. The civilian employees were paid monthly and the calculations of hours-worked etc up to gross wages stage were done for me by the Major. Major was a civilian himself, an Indian who had been doing the job for years and was completely on top of his work. Thinking about it I wonder why he was called Major? It certainly was not his name and he had no official rank. Still Major he was to all of us, RAF personal and civilians alike. A good man, a nice man and he certainly made my job a lot easier.

So calculating the civilian pay and allowances was easy because as I said Major did all the complicated bits. Basically I summarised it, coined up and organised the pay out with the obligatory officer of course. The pay parade was as described for the apprentices except here Major was the verifying officer. I never played any games at this parade as Major took it very seriously and it was the earnings of the civilian staff who had families to keep. The pronunciation of the Kenyan names had posed a problem for some in my job in the past but I found them fairly easy to pronounce. Being used to Welsh pronunciation undoubtedly helped. Several African names started with the letter "n", and this had caused my predecessors untold difficulty but it seemed easy to me. After a few months I was probably better known by the civilian staff than anyone else on camp other than Major. I got some very smart salutes in a joking way around camp especially from the Africans who liked a joke. With my limited knowledge of Swahili, pay queries were interesting and it usually ended up with us sending for Major.

Now I suppose all trades have their own ways of appearing busy while not doing anything and I can only talk for the paper pushers. The tried and tested way for us was to dress reasonably smart, well as smart as everybody else in your khaki shirt, shorts and long socks, carry several bits of paper, preferably on a clip board or in a file, and walk purposefully. I assume all the bosses knew what we were up to but if we looked busy at least they would not get it in the neck from their bosses. Let's face it none of us had much to do anyway. No doubt other trades had their ways but that was ours. So what else happened on camp.

There was a camp cinema. The Astra. Not bad really I suppose. The reproduction quality was good and the films were OK. The Astra was run by some of the airmen on camp and occasionally as a favour I would take over the cash desk duties for a night as relief. Simple job. Man came in. Man handed over cash through little hole in glass partition. Cashier passed over ticket. Man went in to watch film. The first time an apple and an orange came through the hole instead of cash I was a little taken aback, but it was one of the ways a cook got in to see the film. Needless to say you did not issue a ticket on that occasion or balancing up at the end of the night would have been difficult. Bananas were my favourite fruit but I did not get many of them which was a shame.

The buildings on camp were laid out in the standard RAF camp style. Our billet housed twenty men and the billets were grouped around a central toilet block. Most buildings were single storey but a few were of two storey construction. Where they were different from most huts I had been used to were that they were built of dressed stone blocks. They were nice buildings but of course had the steel casement windows and doors. Their construction meant they did not get too hot in the hot season. Inside we were now back to the old fashioned bed with a tall locker and a short locker set up for every airman. A big step down from Weston Super Mare.

A luxury we did enjoy however was having a Dhobi boy clean our room, do our washing and ironing. We all paid him individually, as he was a civilian not a RAF person. They were good and could iron better than I could. During my time we had two Dhobi boys, a silly term for grown men earning a decent living but there you go. The first as I recall was called Hassan. He was very good at cleaning, washing and ironing but was not a very friendly happy man. As we were an occupying force in his country that is not surprising really and he insisted on calling us all bwana, bwana taff to me. I tried to get him to change to calling me taff, but he would not. Our next Dhobi boy was a very cheerful man, always smiling and happy. He became more like a friend than an employee. He had the classic build of a Kenyan runner that we see so often nowadays. Funny though I cannot recall his name although I was closer to him than Hassan. They were both proud of their country however.

The camp had a spacious feel to it as the buildings were well spread out with wide paths and large grass areas. The main roads were bounded by monsoon ditches several feet deep as when it rained in the rainy season it really rained, albeit for only a short time usually. I liked the camp. For me it had a good feel to it.

I previously referred to a childish game we used to play called "getting the officer to salute you first". Simple game really. It worked especially well on Army officers. As you approached one of them you slightly raised you right shoulder. They expecting a salute would throw one up without thinking. You then returned their salute. Great game for the simple minded. The trick was of course to get them to salute you while you made as little a movement of your right arm or shoulder as possible.

You did get some childish people in accounts however. I remember one in Kenya who delighted in pinching you as he passed you at your desk. When the inevitable retaliation happened he squealed like a stuck pig. Bit of a big girl really. It was never him who was at fault of course. Didn't get him many friends though and he seemed to live permanently off camp. Just as well really.

# Chapter Six

## The Falls

I stood there deafened, wet, occasionally almost blinded, awe-struck and lost for words. For ages I just stood and looked. Turning I could see that my companion was similarly fixed to the spot not moving but just taking in the view before us. Yes I had seen pictures of the sight before me, but real life was something different. I looked back and felt a great swelling up inside of me of pride and achievement that I had made it to my destination. Wonder that I had been given the chance to witness this sight. If I looked straight ahead, or up, or down the picture remained the same. A sight of wonder and raw power. Power not created by mankind but the power of nature. Nature in the raw. A power seemingly so immense that it could never be tamed or harnessed. A deafening power so noisy that to talk meant shouting to each other with your mouth almost pressed to your friend's ear. The clarity of the vision ebbed and flowed as the breeze grasped the spray filled air and swirled it around, first taking it away then seemingly wafting it tantalisingly back towards us. Covering us then drifting away. The noisy roar was almost constant, but even that seemed to raise itself to a crescendo then fade away again. But even in these relatively quiet moments to speak was not possible in truth. I wiped my eyes and marvelled again at the view. I had dreamt about this moment for months and now it was here before me in all its magnificent splendour. Victoria Falls.

The two of us were standing on a viewing ledge on the north shore of the falls approximately half way down the chasm into which the falls plunge looking at the Eastern Cataract. We had carefully walked down a narrow path with many steps to reach this place and every step was worth while. The view of Victoria Falls is amazing from any place be it north or south bank, but the feeling of the power of the falls in my view is best grasped from our present vantage point of almost under the falls.

Again I am ahead of myself and really should have started at the beginning but I just could not wait to get the first paragraph down on paper. As I write I still feel the excitement and I can feel a smile crossing my face. Such memories are what living surely is all about. But to remember things, you have to have done them in the first place, and that should be a lesson to us all. If a thing is worth doing, do it now, as the chance might never come again.

I close my eyes and not only can I recall that I was there, looking in awe at Victoria Falls, but I can see it, think that I can hear the roar, and almost smell it.

So what was the beginning of this adventure? Difficult to recall really. Someone must have started the discussion and several of us must have dreamed that we could make this expedition to Victoria Falls a reality. It was about two thousand miles away from where we were so I recall, but of course this was the nearest any of us had been to it before. Looking at the map of Africa now I am still astonished by the distance we covered. We had journeyed about two thirds of the way from Nairobi in Kenya to Cape Town in South Africa. Three of us, only one able to drive, simply had a road map which would not be considered even half adequate today, an old car with no special adaptations, limited cooking and survival supplies. What we did have was an irrepressible desire to get there backed up by supreme confidence, which proved well founded. It is one of the wonders of the world, but we were just airmen with no resources and little money. The RAF would not organise such a trip for us. So how could it happen? Well not easily is the answer I suppose if you look for difficulties, but very easily if you take the relaxed other view. Two of us from the RAF achieved it and I never heard of any others from our camp that did. Perhaps they did not want it as much as we two did.

After the germ of the idea surfaced it was discussed many times with different people. Many were interested initially but fell by the wayside. How would we get there? By bus, by plane, by car? Where would we stay on route and once we got there? So many problems to solve. But the more relaxed view was how great it would be to do this trip, and what is a little hardship to young men. It was the last view that prevailed in the end for two of us. Thinking back it seems improbable that only two of us made the journey in the end. I do not recall why the others did not go as that was their decision and would not affect my trip of a lifetime.

If I was undertaking a trip such as this now I am sure that plans would be drawn up in detail and transport and accommodation booked well in advance. Packing would be a careful exercise and inoculations carefully checked. Well none of those things were done for this trip except the inoculations, but there again with the RAF if you were posted overseas you were injected against everything except stupidity. In the end as the numbers likely to undertake the trip dwindled we had the idea of looking in the local paper to see if anyone was heading south by car and needed passengers to make up the numbers. We would join them on a cost-sharing basis. What happened in the end was that Bill and I went into the AA office in Nairobi and put an advertisement up asking for a lift from anyone going south in the direction of Victoria Falls. For some reason Bill dropped out and I had to recruit another body but Max as it turned out was just as keen as I to go. One evening a few months later into our billet walks a man asking for me. He was going to drive to South Africa and would be glad of the company and someone to share petrol costs as far as we went with him. He would be passing Victoria Falls, which was even better than I had initially hoped for. It was on for September.

The name of our civilian friend was Mick. He was a few years older than we were but not too many. I know the names as they are written on the back of some of the many photos we took on this adventure. Max was in the RAF like me but I cannot now recall exactly what he did there. It did not matter, what mattered was the fact that he too was up for the trip. He too had the desire to go and see the falls. We both booked three weeks leave and hoped that it would be long enough for us to get there and back in time. That we would get there was not in question in our minds. That we would be thrilled by the sights and the experience likewise we took for granted. Whether we would get back before our leave finished was the question, but not too serious a question in reality. To be honest it was not an issue at all, which was just as well because we did not make it back before our leave was up.

I got seven days jankers (extra guard duties, parades and duty clerk shifts) for my absence, Max being a corporal only got a lecture. While I can recall minute details of the exciting part of the trip, I cannot remember much about the jankers. They were probably done while I was still on a high after my experience. My diary recalls that I should have done three parades a day for seven days. In fact I only did nine parades, the equivalent of three days. This was achieved by strategic use of being camp duty clerk on certain days and accounts duty clerk on other days. On these days I was excused parades. As a few of these duties were actually switches with friends the favour to be returned later I did quite well. Another diary note I have to smile at is that I made a profit on the sweep they ran on how bad my punishment would be of £2.50. I always was lucky I suppose.

So we were away. The car a right hand drive Ford Consul registration KBW 18. Looking at my photographs now it looks terribly old fashioned but it got us there. Not without any trouble, but it got us there, and that was all that mattered. The only real problems were punctures and they were fixable. The roads were mostly dirt. Murram was the local name for the material of the roads. They were mostly quite wide and straight. As there were not many villages or towns close together there was no need for them to meander I suppose. The old car did us proud to be fair. Punctures were not just a case of changing the wheel however, the tyre had to come off, the tube patched and then it had to be assembled again. I have several photos of the other two looking frustrated trying to repair punctures. No doubt I was too but of course could not take photos of myself in trouble. Lucky me in hindsight.

The first day we covered 350 miles and planned to stay at a guesthouse. We got there alright but it was full. Slept in the car that night. Second day was a good day apart from the punctures but again it was sleeping in the car for the three of us that night.

The next day we covered a good distance but had to travel in convoy with other traffic due to trouble in the area. Luxury tonight as we slept in a government rest house which meant we had a proper breakfast as well. The following day we covered over 600 miles but again slept in the car just outside Mazabuku.

Regularly we took on fuel, which was another experience. Present day health and safety executives would blow a gasket at the sight of some of the petrol stations we filled up at. The one in my photo is a simple oil drum filled with petrol with a hose leading to a raised glass jar holding one gallon. Another hose ran to the car. First the glass jar was filled from the drum with a hand pump then the contents of the jar was allowed to flow using gravity into the car's petrol tank. Simple, slow but effective and what was the rush anyway? Bit of a problem if you ordered half a gallon too much for your tank though.

Things were not so organised on the return journey but more of that later. Lunch was a more casual affair shall we say. Sometimes a sandwich sometimes a bowl of soup heated over a Primus stove. Sometimes a tin of something heated up. None of us were much in the way of cooks, but we could heat up tins of soup. Our only cooking utensils were a saucepan, a frying pan and a kettle. No motorway pull ins there for us. Just pull off at the side of the road when the driver needed a rest and a quick brew up there and then. If anyone reading this is from Moshi, I was 138 miles from your town in September 1961 on my way south heading for the falls. Got a photo of me and Mick leaning against a road sign to prove it.

To be fair to the roads they were mostly quite good. There were the occasional stretches where they were not, but you never got held up by road works for the very obvious reason that were none. The days passed and if it had not been for the excitement of our trip and the friendly waving of people, especially the children, as we passed, they would have been boring as the scenery while fascinating at first was a little unchanging.

But we arrived on day six tired but safe. Our dream of many months achieved. Getting back when nothing had been organised was a problem for later. Our plan was simply to hitch hike the two thousand miles back to Nairobi. Simple really, but only in theory. But again that is another story. We were there and lived for the moment. We stayed in the Fairmont hotel in Livingstone. While we were there we had decided that we would spend our little money on accommodation and food while saving on transport by walking everywhere. We were reasonably fit and needed to be as we walked for miles. Doing that of course you saw everything and missed nothing.

So back to where I started this chapter. Gazing up at the falls. They do say that the best time to see the falls is outside the rainy season as the spray then blots out the view. I do not know. Certainly when we were there the flow of water was vast, with the spray drifting all around, but the falls could be clearly seen.

It was warm the whole time we were there, my photos show us wearing shirt and shorts all the time, plus when walking in the rain forest a long plastic Mac. This was not protection from the rain but the spray from the falls. We had obviously decided to look smart around the falls and in the hotel as we had changed from our khaki shirts and long trousers into white short sleeved shirts and shorts. I was still sporting my moustache which spoils the image a little but it can only be seen in close ups so is not too much of a disaster. My hair was its customary half-inch long at its longest point with most of it being half that length. Easy to wash. The walks through the jungle/bush around the falls was interesting, while the monkeys were very tame and were always ready to take bits of sandwiches off you.

I have one photo of a Baobab tree. It is massive. You would not believe it could be so big. The only way to appreciate its size is to get a person to stand near it in the photograph. We did this but to take the photo had to walk away from the tree for ever just to get it all in the shot. You then end up having to carefully look for the person in the photo when developed. He is just a spot and there is no way you could recognise who it was. Still everything there was amazing.

What more can I say about the falls. The Main Falls, the Devils Cataract, the Eastern Cataract, Rainbow Falls, the Boiling Pot where you could descend to river level and see the water swirling away from the bottom of the falls. Day after day we walk around them. Some days we again followed the paths to lower levels to enable us to gaze up at them once more. Each day we looked at them in awe. I am sure while we were there I collected statistics on how many tons of water flowed over the falls each minute during the various seasons but such statistics are cold facts. They cannot reflect the reality of seeing it actually happening.

There is a bridge across the ravine just down river of the falls. It is impressive when you consider the place where it is built spanning such a gorge. I have the bare statistics for the bridge as I have a photograph of myself nonchalantly leaning against a sign setting them all out. It was about a mile from our hotel, and was constructed in 1905 by an engineering firm from Darlington. The height above the water at low level is 411 feet but only 355 feet at high water. The main span is some 500 feet. Statistics do not do the bridge justice.

One day we took a river boat ride above the falls. Thankfully the coxswain did not take us too close to the top. The river is wide and even during the non rainy season deep and powerful. The green of the jungle reaching right down to the waters edge added to the wildness of the scenery. A lone Hippopotamus, a large beast to be given ample room, swam past. The birds in the jungle were multi coloured and noisy, and of course the inevitable monkeys displayed themselves. A wonderful half-day but tame compared with viewing the actual falls.

We of course did the normal tourist sight seeing visits to Livingstone's monument and the Rhodes-Livingstone Museum, both well kept, preserved and interesting. We ate well during our stay as something told us we might not have such an easy return journey, and so it turned out.

# Chapter Seven

## Return To Nairobi

At last we decided it was time to head back. Goodbye Victoria Falls, hallo the open road. Two thousand miles to go and the only plan was that we were going to hitch hike the whole way staying in as cheap accommodation as we could find each night. What this would be depended on who gave us a lift. Our map was basic and our plans did not include any fixed destinations to reach each night but rather the plan was to hope for the best and see what turns up each day and night. It worked for a while as well.

Now I should here explain a few basic points about hitch hiking in East Africa, although by now I suppose it was not east Africa but more like central South Africa. Still the rules and who were likely to give you lifts remained the same. Obvious rule one get outside the town or village you are in and stand at the side of the road you intend travelling along. Sounds basic but I can remember that once one RAF man went the wrong way for quite a while north of Nairobi because he hitched on the wrong road. How he achieved that I cannot understand as surely he asked where the driver was going before getting in. Still I did say earlier that there was no inoculation for stupidity didn't I. He proved it.

Who was likely to give you lifts was also forecastable. Former Europeans were always likely to stop, so were many Africans of European stock. Native Kenyans were always good for a lift I found although generally they were not going as far and had slower vehicles. There were also fewer of them with transport. Asians and Kenyans of Asian stock were less likely to give lifts. I never found out the reason and it made no sense to me as on an individual basis I got on with them well. Still you always had to remember it was the other person's vehicle and it was their choice if they gave you a lift or not. They owed you nothing and indeed it was you who were in their debt after any lift. They did not look on it as a debt to be repaid, most did it for the company and conversation on route.

So off we went and at first it was very good. By the traffic levels of the area the traffic was quite good and lifts materialised. Some were short and some quite reasonable distances and time and distance passed.

The first night we got as far as Mazabuku but the hotel was full and we finally spent the night in a police station. There was no formal accommodation anywhere in the village other than the hotel and sleeping under the stars with not even a tent for protection did not appeal. A night in the cells did appeal by comparison. The police would not give us a cell for the night however but to be fair to them did not completely turn us away either. They let us sleep in an office for the night. Now offices do not have beds, and we did not carry any equipment, not even a sleeping bag. The result? How do you fancy sleeping on a bare table? Well I can tell you it gets hard as the night wears on but it is better than the floor as at least snakes do not climb on top of tables. The next day lifts were hard to come by and the miles dragged. We were stuck out in the open road again as dusk approached and our plan was to sleep in the back of an open truck parked nearby. We were saved by a tobacco farmer who put us up for the night. He lived in an old African shaped hut but it was well furnished and clean. We were lucky, no back of truck.

Next day we only managed 70miles and got to Serenje. Tonight we slept in a government rest house. Luxury again. There is more trouble now in Katanga in the Congo the border of which is very close. Traffic was even less than before.

We reached Mpika and are now running late. Road was fantastically quiet I write in my diary.

We decided that, as progress had to be made to travel by local bus for a while. It was forecast to cover 150miles each day for the next two days which would be good going compared with what we had been reduced to. Cost forty-two shillings. Now that was another real experience. One we had not planned to make but certainly well worth having done. We boarded the bus early in the morning but it was already packed and all the seats appeared full. No problem. Everybody just squeezed up a little tighter so that we could sit down. When the bus left there was hardly enough room to breathe inside. It did not travel very quickly as it was so heavily loaded but it progressed slowly in the right direction. There was a definite language barrier between us and the rest of the passengers, but between using sign language, my limited Swahili and getting the help of those who could speak a little English we actually had an interesting time. We were on the bus for two whole days heading towards Mbeya. It was a bus of the Central African Road line, registration BH 6214. Piled high on top with luggage and crammed with us inside.

We stopped occasionally for people to get off but more frequently it appeared for even more to get on. Each time a new passenger got on our presence was explained to them and we were openly gazed at, especially by the children. It was a curiosity for so called white people to travel on this bus. You could not have had more friendly fellow travellers. At each stop for a drink or food we were shown where to find water etc. If for some reason we did not get off when most others did water was offered to us. The less shy ones were desperately trying to make conversation with us, you would have thought we were back home in Wales, where talking to strangers on the bus or train is normal practice. It was some of the very young children I remember best. Some eventually plucked up enough courage to touch our so-called white skin. Now to be fair although we had good dark tans we were a lot paler than they were, and all children no matter where are naturally curious.

So two days on the bus making very slow progress. The first night we were directed to an official type guesthouse in Isolo. Some luxury again after a day on the bus. But early next morning we were away again. Some fellow travellers were our friends of the day before and some were new. The examination of these strange fellow passengers continued again throughout the day. That night the bus journey was over and we were again staying in a guesthouse in Mbeya.

Up early next morning with renewed vigour and back to plan one, to hitch the rest of the way. Disastrous day. Not even a lift of one mile. There just was no traffic at all going our way. After a very hot sweaty day by the side of the road and having not gained a single foot towards our destination back we trudge to the guesthouse of last night. Another comfortable night then out early again by the side of the road. Same result. No traffic at all going our way. So back once more to the guesthouse.

The news was that traffic was just not moving because of the problems over the border. We were now overdue and so were AWOL. We decide that night that if we do not get a lift by mid day we would try to book a flight from the small local airport to Nairobi. Next morning up early and again no luck by noon. The choice was now to continue with the apparently hopeless attempt to get a lift or book a flight. The flight won, as we still had six hundred miles to go. The first flight was in two days time. To get the money for the flight we telephoned the camp and asked for money to be transferred to the local bank as an advance of pay. So back to the guesthouse we go.

We did not bother to try for a lift next day but spent it exploring a hill near the guesthouse. To call it a hill is a little unkind as it reached 9,200feet above sea level. It was a good long walk but the view looking down from the summit was fantastic. You could see for miles. Walking in the sun did not seem as tiring as just sitting by the side of the road waiting for something that did not happen, and was much more enjoyable.

Its Wednesday and our flight is due to leave. Does not happen due to engine problem with plane. Back to the guesthouse. Its Thursday and we are to leave. At Mbeya they refuelled the plane with a hand pump which seemed a little lax but at our next stop they actually filled the tanks straight out of three gallon drums. Still it worked. We landed at Dar-es-salaam and Mombassa then Nairobi. Taxi from airport to camp and straight to the guardroom to report. We were just logged in and told to report next day to our squadron commander.

While we had not completed the trip as we had planned, we had done it under our own steam with our own motivation and no official help. The trip was amazing and our sense of achievement great. We had done something that the thousands of others there did not do to the best of my knowledge, certainly not in the way we did it. The sights and the actual adventure can never be forgotten. It was a trip to beat all trips.

# Chapter Eight

## Sport

Sport played a big part in the life of many of us in the forces in Kenya. Not that most of us were any good at any sport in particular but the opportunities were there so we took them. At least the people I became friendly with did. I suppose like tends to attract like in all fields of life. Some sports I had played before but others I had never heard of let alone played.

### Squash

Squash to me was a drink. To make it you added water to a thick syrup like liquid. But no, I now found out that it was a game where you hit a small ball against a wall repeatedly, taking turns with your opponent to hit it. You were not supposed to try to hit your opponent with either the ball or your racket, nor were you supposed to try to knock him over. And tackling was a complete no, no. It was generally played by two people of the same sex in a small room with no windows. At least the lights were on. Now to someone like me, who had led a sheltered life, this sounded like either a wind up, a real tall tale, or some type of Masonic ceremony. On finding out the court was situated behind the officers mess and that to play you had to walk into the officers mess to get the key, I was even more convinced that it was some sort of initiation ceremony.

But I tried it. I liked it to. I was always just one step up from completely useless at squash even on my good days but I enjoyed it as a game. I am not really a bat and ball man. Of course if you play with someone of your own level, that is poor, you can have a good game at squash. My best opponent was Jock, he was of the same standard as me.

He had a sports car and saved me from getting my head cut off on one occasion, but again that is a story for later.

My strengths at squash were my fitness. I could run around the court all day. Also my seeming ability to bounce myself off the walls without causing myself any damage, as often as I bounced the ball off the walls. If Jock is reading this and can remember me I played squash a few years ago and am still no better. Incidentally the ball, little though it is can really hurt if it hits you direct from your opponent's racket. Still a good game.

## Cricket

Still thinking about sport, I was never much of a cricket fan. Girls game really, and not for sporting girls either. Just turned a couple of readers into enemies I suppose, but say it as you find it. Before my Kenya days I had played cricket in an organised game only once in my life and that was one day in school. I liked athletics, and that usually clashed with cricket, and when it didn't I tried to make it clash by volunteering for an extra training run or something. The day I played in school I stayed on the boundary out of the way so some people probably thought I was not even in the game but was just watching. So why did I play in the RAF? Well it was only once and then mostly due to blackmail. Thinking back that Flight Sergeant in accounts cannot say anything about my light workload, as he still owes me a pint of beer for winning the cricket match. Implausible though it might sound I did win the match for my team. Admin. Wing was a man short and I was lying idly at the side of the pitch, doing nothing and minding my own business and so got volunteered

They were playing Tech Wing. A boastful lot, especially the NCO's, and our Flight Sergeant desperately wanted to beat them. I suppose I was a better option than nothing, so into the team I was drafted. Wisely during their innings I was sent out to the boundary out of harm's way. I suppose you could call this my specialised position as I played there in all my cricket matches, both of them that is. If you wanted to be less kind I suppose there are other things you could say. Apparently they thought even I could stop the ball and throw it back to the wicket keeper: can't remember the score but as our innings progressed we were not doing too well. They had a fast bowler who I was told was very fast and this was our downfall. Now if you knew much about cricket this might have meant something but at the time it did not mean much to me. You can by now guess that I was not selected as the opening batsman. No, it was number eleven for me. I was happy with that position as well. Sadly however when eventually it came to my turn we still needed runs, about ten if I recall correctly. Out I walk a bit like a duck in these strange pads and gloves. Just before I walked out, our by now distraught Flight Sergeant says to me, "if you win this for us Taff I'll buy you a pint". Now to be kind to him he was the type of man who could not help having been born with short arms, though I suppose he did not have to buy trousers with deep pockets. You get the type of man he was? Now to get him to buy a drink for someone was a real challenge. Cricket had suddenly taken on a new light as far as I was concerned. It had now become a real sport. One worth taking part in. So out I march, proper cricketer now, ready to take on this fast bowler even if they had not given me a bat.

As I have said before I am not a great one for hand, eye, bat and ball co-ordination, I prefer rugby and athletics, so I knew that it would be pointless me trying to hit this bowler all over the place in a scientific manner. What I had to do was stop him knocking over my wicket, while running between the wickets whenever possible. Now to be fair I was helped by this bowler. Instead of trying to just bowl me out, probably not too difficult to do, he must have thought he could have fun with me and frighten me off. My plan, remember, was to stand there with the bat in front of the wicket and hope for the best. We were now talking serious sport as there was a pint resting on the outcome of my performance. I still remember it vividly now. The ball was red and seemed very large. Larger than I had expected. It was also easy to follow its flight strange as it might seem. The first ball was obviously going to be too high to hit the wickets and was going to hit me in the body. Well that's OK I thought, that won't get me out. And of course it didn't. I seemed happier than the bowler did after this happened twice. The next one not only missed the wicket it even missed me, and we ran two runs. I was now starting to enjoy this game, as the prospect of free beer at the expense of old short arms loomed nearer.

Now to be honest I only hit the ball twice. Once apparently I was told was a very good shot. The ball pitched in line with the wicket was low and very near where I placed the foot of the bat on the ground. I blocked the ball and it rolled harmlessly a few feet away in front of me. My other contact was a wild slash at a ball well wide of the off stump. The bowler was getting more erratic by now. Apparently I just made contact and it flew well away from all those fielding. We ran two more. All the others came from extras, which we ran when the ball seemed far enough away for us not to get run out. Certainly not by intention, as I did not realise then that there were only six balls per over and after that they bowled from the other end, I seemed to always be receiving the bowling. Another scrambled run and we had won, but I never did get that pint from old deep pockets.

## Athletics

Now athletics had always been my main summer sport. I still recall now my mother, who was smarter than your average bear when it came down to it, getting me to do small amounts of shopping by asking me to "run" up the shop for her. I am sure that if I had been asked to "walk" up the shop for her, or "go" up the shop for her, while I would have gone, I went much happier because I had been asked to "run" up the shop. As a child I had always wanted to race against the other children. That is not to say I always won but loved the race. We had no fancy oval tracks where I came from. Indeed the nearest we came to having a track was to run around the local football field grandly named Hendreforgan Park, or to the locals "The Ash Tip" because that is what it was, a converted refuse tip. The odd broken bottle or tin can came through to the surface occasionally but it was "Our Ash Tip".

So as you would expect when the RAF planned to enter a team in a long distance relay race along the coast of Kenya I was there ready to join the team. To be fair when you think that I thought a good way to pass part of an evening would be to go out for an eight or ten mile run around the camp then I was a likely team member. Distance running, alone in the countryside, is a very relaxing physical and mentally invigorating thing to do. At the first meeting I knew it would not work.

The race was to be over a fair distance, seventy-three miles to be run by a relay of six or eight runners. It never happened though.

The biggest talker there propounded the theory that what we needed was several sprinters who would run two hundred yards very quickly to build up a lead and that if we dropped behind they would again be introduced to bridge any gap. The man was an obvious dummy when it came to running and tactics, and as you will have guessed was, or he at least thought he was, a sprinter. It turned out I was as fast as he was anyway even in a sprint, which was not surprising as my two rugby positions were wing and wing forward. I was never the fastest but I had the legs of this man. As it happened Kenya was overtaken by severe flooding before the race took place so it was abandoned much to my relief. While I would have relished the race I could not have stuck having dummy in our team. More about those floods later. I was delighted and proud to have been involved in the supply of food to those people cut off by the floods. The most memorable lesson for me that came from this proposed race however was how little you can believe of what you read in the newspapers.

In the lead up to the race the Nairobi newspapers were full of talk about this dark horse team being entered by the RAF. Yes it was us they were talking about. They had obviously not been at any of our team meetings. The story was that we had the advantage of coming down from living at altitude and racing at sea level. Yes it works with highly trained athletes but for our rabble it was a joke. Now I am a great admirer of Kenyan distance and middle distance athletes, and to be fair they were not so developed then as they are now, but us to beat them? Definitely a joke. Still it probably sold newspapers, which was the object of the exercise for them.

# Chapter Nine

## Nairobi Game Park

To someone who had only seen wild animals in a zoo the game parks were wonderful. Remember there were no fancy game parks in the UK then. To see the animals in their real surroundings close up was the experience of a lifetime. To do such trips now, as a tourist is an expensive business and there was I able to do it any weekend. Worth being a regular to get to Kenya and do this. Nature programmes on television from game parks are great, but to be there, hastily shutting a car window as a lion walks up to the car and looks in is something else when you can almost smell its breath. Seeing a pride of lions tearing apart some other animal from close up, while in a way it was gruesome, it was also exciting, as remember they were not fed artificially at all, but had to hunt for their food. It really was nature in the raw. To watch a lion just walking past your car window is an amazing experience. They are so graceful yet powerful and arrogant. A truly marvellous beast.

Zebras and Wildebeest grazed the park like sheep on my native Rhondda Mountains. They were everywhere. More wary than the lion, but they were the hunted not the hunter. I always smiled when I saw my first Zebra of the day, as it seemed to be like a fat short-legged pony. They always seemed well fed, smartly dressed and tidy. The Wildebeest however always seemed lean, scraggy and untidy, scruffy even if you can say that about an animal. They always looked as if they had dressed in a hurry that morning and had not had time to wash and shave.

Giraffe were strange animals. Perfectly designed to feed on the topmost leaves of the trees but they appeared clumsy when forced to run, and very clumsy when stooping down to drink with their front legs splayed wide apart. They were not to be argued with by man though.

There was a tale, whether true or not I do not know, about the giraffe that lived near the road through the rift valley between Nairobi and Nakuru. He allegedly would stand in the road if he felt like it and woe betides any car that upset him. Their radiator soon came off second best to his rear hoof.

While on the topic of game parks I must tell you of the time our gang of intrepid (stupid) adventurers were thrown out of the game park by the rangers. They told us we were banned for a year but that did not seem to work as we were back within a few weeks. I suppose they were just trying to frighten us that's all. It all came about when one of us, and I don't think it was me this time, thought it would be great to have photographs of the animals running towards us and leaping over us. Brilliant idea. So next weekend off we go to the game park armed with cameras, drinks and sandwiches for a serious day of action photography.

The plan was simple. Two of the gang could drive so we hired a self-drive VW minibus. Up very early that morning, quick breakfast and away. The reserve was not very far way and we soon arrived there. Several miles into the park when it seemed that no one else was around, we selected a herd of various animals, zebra, wildebeest, Thompson gazelle etc. and being clever, or so we thought, we drove down wind of them till we found a suitable gully. All except the driver climbed quietly out. Now I should add at this stage that this is strictly against the rules of the game park except in certain areas because people taste nice to some animals whether they are cooked or raw. Still out we got. Crept into the ditch and selected good camera positions. We settled down to wait while the driver of the VW drove around behind the herd taking the long way around. Remember you do not have to stay on the roads in a game park in the dry season, as it is just wild open country where the animals have right of way. Anyway our driver started to herd the animals towards us making them move as fast as he could.

Now we come to the bit where we begin to doubt who are the smartest, the animals or us. I think we came second. They just would not run towards us but set off at right angles to the way we wanted them to go. No dramatic photos of leaping animals for us. But then another type of animal appears. Much more fierce than a zebra. A game warden. We do not take photos of this wild animal but try to look all innocent. That failed as well. Justifiably I suppose, but none too politely, he suggests that we get back in our vehicle, give him our names, rank, number and squadron, and leave his game park with all due haste. While I cannot recall his exact words they did go along those lines. He did point out to us as he escorted us from the park where the nearest lions were, and that did dampen our enthusiasm for getting out of our vehicles on future ventures in game parks as they were very near where we had tried to take our action photos.

We visited game parks many times and each time it was a wonderful experience. Elephants are huge but so graceful. While they could just ignore everything and simply walk where they felt like, they actually seemed to gently pick their way around things. A rhino on the other hand gives the impression that it will charge right through anything just because it was there. The herds of zebra, wildebeest and hartebeest, the graceful gazelle of various types, monkeys, ostrich, waterbuck, large eland and wild pigs all an experience to be enjoyed.

Governments preserving our planet's wild life by setting aside areas of land for them to live in naturally should be supported by us all. Mankind does not have the right to cause the extinction of any other form of life. Now of course it is made a little easier for these countries as they earn good revenue from tourists coming to see the wild animals, but then it was much less profitable and I would suggest therefore not only harder to do but more noble.

# Chapter ten

## Flood relief

I mentioned earlier the floods that prevented the long distance relay race taking place. While for most of the year it was dry and sunny in Kenya they did have a rainy season, which was very predictable. This year however there were floods and many people were cut off from all supplies. An airdrop of basic grains was organised jointly by the civilian authorities, the RAF and the army air dispatch group. The army did not have enough manpower to keep the drop going all the daylight hours day after day and so volunteers were called for from the RAF. Now forget what you have heard about volunteering. If it sounds like fun, or sounds worthwhile it probably is, so volunteer. At least that was my motto. It did not always work out and occasionally you ended up doing an extra guard duty, but mostly it worked out OK. You only get one go in this life so they tell me. So I volunteered. I got great satisfaction from doing it, felt it was worthwhile, enjoyed myself, and it was a change from the stresses of my normal job!

Basically the operation was that the civilian authorities delivered the hundred weight sacks of grain to the Nairobi airfield where it was stored. We loaded it into RAF Beverly aeroplanes, which were slow flying transport planes. We then flew over the cut off areas and threw the sacks out, returned to the airfield and did it again until it went dark. Stopped then started again at daybreak and continued till the floods went down and the roads were passable again.

In more detail the operation involved the army dispatchers and the RAF volunteers, assisted by civilians, humping these hundred weight sacks into the aeroplane and stacking them safely so that the load would not shift while we were in flight. The plane then took off and while it flew to our drop zone we all had a cuppa. On arrival we loaded the rear ramp with the designated number of sacks. We then stood there waiting for the droplights to signal the drop should be made. On the green light we lifted the inner side of the ramp and the sacks just fell out of the rear of the plane onto the drop zone. We were doing the drop from a height of 50feet. That is low. From that height you could see the expressions on the people's faces and see the bags bouncing. We stood there on the rear edge of the plane just looking down as if it was an everyday occurrence. I suppose for the army men it was. To be fair we were attached to the plane by a safety harness. Mostly that is, but I will return to the time the harness was not attached in a moment.

The plane would circle around while we frantically worked to load the drop board again with more sacks, we then went through the same procedure as before, including waving to those on the ground. Very few of the sacks broke as it had been calculated apparently that if we dropped them at the right speed from the right height they would remain intact. Seemed to work anyway.

It was heavy hard work with long hours but was worthwhile we all felt and therefore we enjoyed it.

Meal times were good. We ate at somebody's expense, not ours, at the civilian airfield. This was after the cut backs had been made in our own canteen on camp so these meals were more appreciated than ever. Looking back we must have fancied ourselves as we kept our safety harness on at all times even when on the ground, probably trying to look like some modern day heroes. They were not hot to wear, as they were just a simple full body webbing harness with safety hooks on the end of a long webbing strap to attach yourself to secure fastening points with.

I have just been looking at some photos of the crew I was with during this operation. We are shown loading the one millionth pound of grain onto the aircraft. You can see by the way that we are all gathered around the opening looking at the sack that it is a carefully posed photo. We all have our caps on and shirts done up etc. Nothing like it really was when we were doing it for real. Surprise, surprise who is in the centre of the photo, yes you guessed it, me. Probably the most junior person there. Remember what I said about believing what you see in newspapers. This time though I suppose it was a fair way to take the photo especially with me in the centre. Max from my Victoria Falls trip is in the photo as well. Obviously another who liked volunteering.

Now let's return to the occasion when one of the harnesses was not attached to its safety clip on the floor of the aircraft. We were waiting for the signal to drop another load of sacks when the loader next to me saw that one of our harness hooks had become unattached to its fixing. He called on everyone to stay quite still while he traced it back to the now unattached loader. It was me. No problem and I was soon reattached but if it had not been noticed and I had slipped the best I could have hoped for was to be eating the local food for a few weeks in the middle of the floods. Let it just be said that after that I was always making doubly sure that I was always attached firmly to the appropriate mounting.

Eventually our work was completed and I returned to pay accounts and a right rollicking. I had forgotten to tell my NCO what I was doing and they had lost track of me. They thought I had gone AWOL. (Absent without leave). Definitely thick regular this time not clever national service man. As I had been AWOL once before while on my trip to Victoria Falls, failing to get back on time, I suppose you cannot blame them. Still as it had not interfered with my civilian pay work I was let off with just a rocket and a warning.

Funny really because if I had been in the army dispatch company I would have earned my dispatcher's wings to wear on my uniform, but as a RAF body I did not qualify. So no wings, just a telling off. As with my time in Aden I failed to get any decoration on a technicality, but as I said before, I was not a collector of gongs, so no problem.

# Chapter Eleven

## Mosquitoes, bed bugs and snakes

Now not all the wild animals in Kenya were large and fierce. Some were small and fierce. And of the three I am going to talk about, I am not sure if technically they are even animals, but that does not matter amongst friends does it? First, Bed Bugs and Mosquitoes. Creatures of the night who ate the unwary or the unprepared. It was often said that "if the bed bugs didn't get you the mossies would". Now our RAF camp in Kenya was 5,000 feet plus above sea level so for most of the year the mosquitoes were not a problem and even when they were about there were not many and they seemed harmless. It did depend on who you were. Some people were affected, others were not bothered by the mossies. It depended what you tasted like it was said. I believe now that garlic and the tonic drunk with gin repels mossies but I did not use either then, and they did not appear to like the taste of me. They came at night when you were in bed and all was quiet. Even in a billet of twenty-two men it eventually gets quiet. You would lie there hearing the buzzing sound of their wings and knew you were safe. Then the buzzing stopped and you knew they had landed. The strike was about to happen. As I said though they did not seem to bother to land on me and if they did, they did not bite. So no problem.

We all had mosquito nets hanging on the wall at the head of our beds which we could pull down each night, tuck the ends under our mattress and then you were protected from mossies. Unfortunately the bed bugs lived in the top of the mosquito nets. This meant you had to regularly check your nets to find and kill the bed bugs before they had a chance to get at you. Miss one and in the morning you had the bites to show where they had sucked out your blood. Not painful but they itched. Your only revenge was to try to find the bug, which was now round and bloated with your blood and kill it. When you tried to kill them before they had fed you had to crush them between the nails on you fingers as they were flattish. After they had fed all you needed to do was crush them between the flesh of your fingers they were that fat. It might seem cruel to kill them like this but it was your blood.

I found that the bed bugs would bite me so I never bothered with the mosquito net, it was much easier and less effort.

Down on the coast things were different however. There the mosquitoes carried malaria and while they did not appear to like the taste of me down there either; it was not worth taking the chance so I used the nets. Get mossies trapped inside your net however and you were in trouble. They are not big and if they land on a white meshed mosquito net they are almost impossible to see. But a mosquito trapped inside your net has nothing to do but bite. Still there were much nastier crawlies about in Kenya. Snakes.

Now I do not like snakes. It might be illogical as many are harmless, but I do not like them. To be fair I did not see many in Kenya but the twice I did, they certainly improved my sprinting speed. If I had kept going and been timed over 100 metres I would have easily broken the world record by a significant margin even slowing down towards the end. The twice I saw snakes close up they could not have been closer. In both cases I stopped because someone said, “Snake”. I looked down and there was the friendly little thing lying between my feet. In both cases I did not carefully look to see what type of snake it was for later discussion, I took off.

The first time we were on camp just walking along the road. One of my friends said, “Snake”, which gets you to stop very quickly, as you do not want to step on one. Neither to hurt it nor annoy it into attacking. I looked down and there it was. As I did not stop there long I cannot say if it was a plain or pretty snake but recall that it was not very long. The second occasion was when we were out on a very long walk around the rim of an extinct volcano, Longonot. We were walking around the actual rim when the call snake went up. And stone me if there wasn’t a snake lying between my feet again. Swift exit stage right for yours truly. Surprisingly those were the only two occasions I saw snakes close up in the whole of my two years in Kenya and I did quite a lot of walking in the countryside and bush. Just as well as I still do not like snakes. I remember on the occasion when I saw the snake on the Longonot walk one of my companions was much braver than I was, or much more foolish in my view attacked he snake with the strap of his camera. The snake slid off onto the scrub but in my view he took a great chance, as I am sure if it had wanted to it could have moved quicker than he could. As you will have gathered I did not observe his heroics from close up but from a very safe distance.

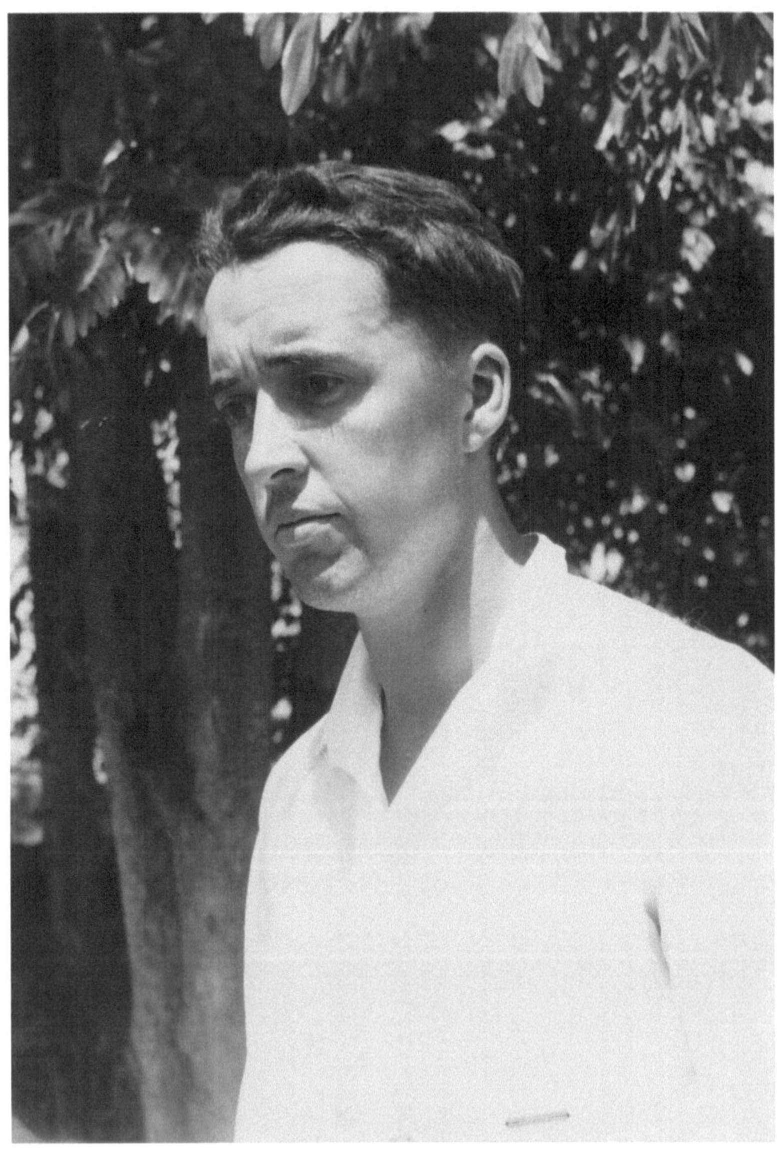

The Author 1961

R.A.F. Bridgenorth - Square bashing December 1958 / January 1959

Author middle row extreme right

Royal Air Force  Hereford.

No. 2 School of Admin. Trades.

Vivian of Hereford.

No. 4/59 BASIC CLERK ACCOUNTING COURSE From 12-2-59 To 25-3-59.

AC's Lawrence Atherton Mumby Love Hill Field Mears

AC's Hall Bonser Cafferky Cooper Mears Reeves Weir Howard

AC's Dandy Bryant Cpl Medland Flt. Lt. J.A. Calvert AC's Fossett Denman Tanner

Instructor. Flt. Cmmdr. Senior man.

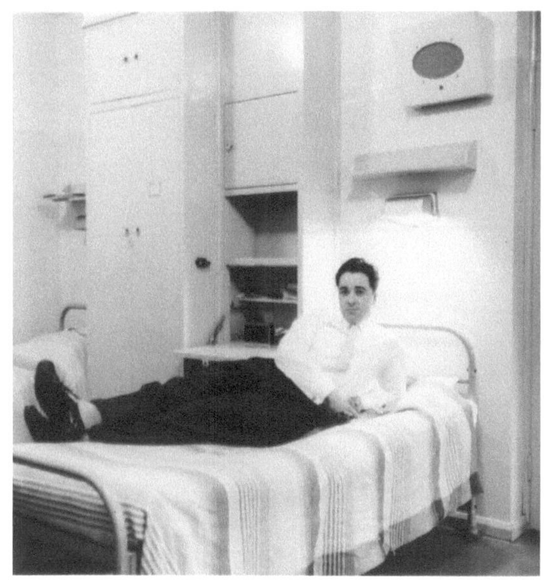

R.A.F. Locking - Weston Super Mare. My "pit" only 4 to a room 1959

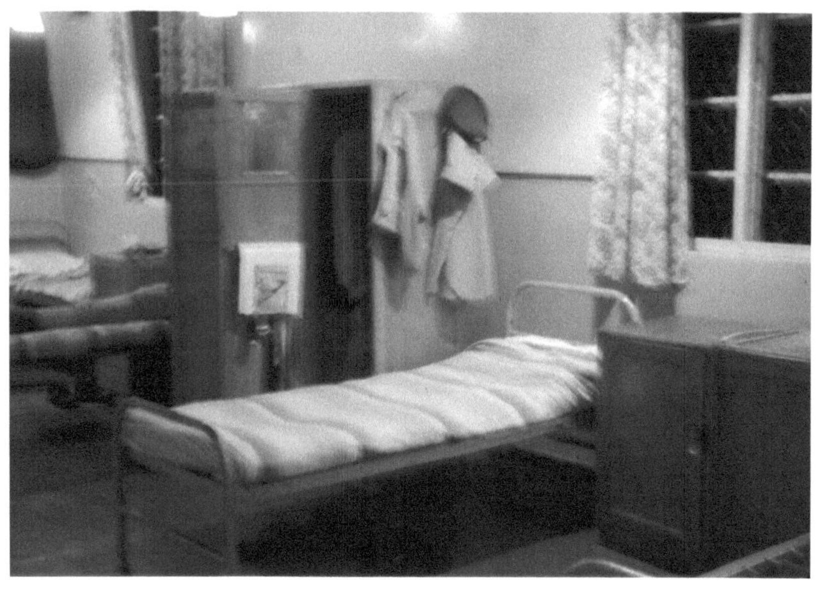

R.A.F. Eastleigh , Kenya. My "pit", back to normal 20 to a room plus basic lockers

Victoria Falls Expedition. Our car at a "very " basic petrol station 1961.

Victoria Falls Expedition. We spent two days on the bus on return journey 1961

Author at Victoria Falls

Eastern catarract - Victoria Falls

Author (extreme left) and friends after being thrown out of Nairobi Game Park.
From left Malcom, Max (who was on Victorian Falls expedition) Pete and Spike. 1961.

Author Nairobi Game Park Kenya 1961

Flood relief Kenya 1961. Author (centre and smiling). One millionth pounds sack being loaded onto Beverly aircraft

Flood relief Kenya 1961. View from rear of aircraft just after drop

Longonot Peak 1961

Suntanned author Mombasa 1960

Mosque in old Arab quarter, Mombasa 1961

Author with "billet" pets 1961. (Actualy at Carr Hartleys animal sanctuary.)

Carr Hartleys 1961

Author wounded in action ?

Author at altitude on Equator 1960

Author on the road 1961 Kenya

Thika Falls , Kenya 1961

Author, porter and another climber. Kilimanjaro 1961.
Mwanze peak in background.

Author on Kilimanjaro 1961. Kibo peak in background

Flood relief - Beverly aircraft 1961.

# Chapter Twelve

## Longonot Crater

I mentioned Longonot crater when I was talking about snakes. The crater is an extinct volcano in the Rift Valley. It is approximately fifty miles from Nairobi on the road to Nakuru. I went there several times, as I liked the wildness of the landscape. It was not pretty in what most people think of as the accepted sense, but I loved its wildness. You could call it grey and drab I suppose but beauty is in the eye of the beholder they say and I liked that area. It was dusty and dry but we enjoyed our walks there. We hitched the fifty or so miles there from Nairobi, drove down the escarpment into the rift valley and got dropped off at the point nearest to the crater. It was some way off the road but the walk while dusty was good. There was just a trail across the open countryside to the foot of the crater.

I suppose the trail was an animal track which wandered about a bit but went in the right general direction. There were no trees there just bushes, and at the times we walked there they were mainly brown with very little green. It all depended on the time of the year and the rainfall. There was very little in the way of wildlife either which considering the scarcity of the vegetation was not surprising. Once we reached the foot of the crater the path went up steeply and the serious walking started. I was told the top was over nine thousand feet high. We were young and fit so it is hard to gauge now how difficult a walk it was. It certainly was a fair height above the surrounding plain and you could see for miles once you reached the top.

The crater was about two miles across, with this narrow animal type track circling its rim. The edge of the crater was not even but rose and fell with the highest point marked as the summit by a concrete filled drum with a post sticking out of the top and of course a sign. I have often wondered who bothered to take this equipment, all be it very primitive, to the top just to mark it. Still not to complain, it was something to have your photo taken against. I am no expert on volcanoes but this seemed a large crater to me so it would have been impressive in its day.

After a complete circle of the rim of the crater, which took about three hours, we then retraced our steps back to the road. There we just stood and waited for a lift the fifty or so miles back to Nairobi. While there was never much traffic on the road we always got a lift without waiting a long time. People travelled long distances there, simply because there were long distances between places. They often travelled alone or in just pairs and so seemed to appreciate the different conversation a hitchhiker could provide.

We always carried plenty of water and sometimes a few sandwiches or fruit but basically nothing else except a camera. Weather conditions there did not change quickly to catch you out, and if it had rained, which it never did on any of our Longonot expeditions, it would have been nice warm rain, so no worry there. The trips were always worthwhile just to see and experience being out in genuinely wild country.

My motto was that if you had been taken what seemed like half way round the world you should get out there and see the country. And what a country Kenya was so see!

At the side of the Escarpment road was an interesting little church built I was told during the Second World War, by Italian prisoners of war, who were employed on constructing the Escarpment road.

While in this area we also visited Lake Naivasha, which you could see from the rim of Longonot crater, and conversely gave a good view of the crater from the lake.

# Chapter Thirteen

## World Bed Push Attempt

Picture the scene. Dusk has come and gone. It is now almost completely dark. You are walking alone along a lonely tarmac road through the countryside. There are no lights near at hand but you can see the distant lights of houses flickering. All is quiet. All is still. You are alone in a solitary part of Kenya. The birds and most animals have retired for the night. The night hunters are not yet on the prowl. You walk on through the silence, undisturbed. The silence is almost oppressive. The only sound is the noise of your solitary footsteps on the tarmac. You can hear your own breath and feel your own heart beat. You are relaxed and at peace. It is cool after the heat of the day and there is not a breath of wind.

A distant rumble catches your ears then dies away again. Moments later you hear it again. Was it nearer this time? You stop to listen. It disappears. Moments later it is back, before fading again to nothing. A sound mirage? Is that possible? You walk on again. Now it is back louder this time and appears nearer. The rumble is accompanied by a slapping sound and what appears to be the agonised breathing of a wild animal. Again you stop. Your emotions? Curiosity? Fear? The sound fades away yet again. You stay fixed to the spot ready now for instant flight. The noises are back, louder than before, more frightening as they increase in volume. You step off the road and crouch to make yourself smaller.

Suddenly the noise is much greater magnified by the silence of the night and then it appears almost on top of you. A ghostly object, dark, square, menacing, with two high points to the rear. It roars nearer and is suddenly level with you, sweeps past, a strange form with two ghostly figures attached to its rear, then disappears again into the blackness of the night, the sounds of its passing swiftly receding to nothing. The night is calm and quiet once more. You straighten up and try to calm your fast beating heart.

"It's those damn bed push people out training after dark with no lights again" you swear to yourself.

I was one of those who in 1960 were training to break the world bed push record.

The story starts as all good stories start over a few pints of beer. I will state now that this is a completely true story, although even I seem to have doubts at times as it seems too far fetched, but I was there and was one of the main participants.

The wacky co-ordinator was a corporal who was a classic fixer. If any of you have seen the musical Miss Saigon he would have been The Engineer. He was overweight and hated exercise for himself but not for other people. He was a great talker and persuader of people, although this talent did wane when you came to know him better, but he would not do anyone any harm. It was his idea that we would get up a team from the RAF in Kenya to break the world bed push record. He was to be the non-active manager. He would organise the equipment, arrange the event, so that the record would be recognised in the Guinness Book of Records, and arrange all the other details.

Myself and one of my closest friends were the two main stalwarts of his team of pushers. We were to carry out the physical testing of the bed, select the other team members and arrange the training schedules of the whole team. As my main hobby seemed to be running around the camp and my close friend John, while not so fanatical was also blessed with quite a lot of stamina we joined in enthusiastically.

The "Engineer" actually talked the Matron of the local hospital, or so he told us, into lending us a hospital bed. Where it came from I was never sure but arrive it did, and it was a hospital bed. Sturdy with wheels about four inches across and with a heavy slab instead of springs as we were used to with service beds. He had also agreed with one of the men on camp, an ex jockey apprentice, to be the "patient" during the world record attempt. He was small and light, ideal, as we did not want to push a greater weight than was necessary. During training it was agreed that he would not be on the bed but that we would leave the heavy centre of the bed on in his place. We could therefore train with a heavy bed but for the actual record attempt would reduce the weight as much as possible, while making sure that the bed would not fall apart and that our "patient" would be able to stay in it.

Testing commenced. The two of us pushing the bed around the two mile road surrounding the main part of the camp. The first problem was control of the direction of the bed. It behaved like a demented supermarket trolley, although in those days I did not know what a supermarket trolley was like, or even if they had been invented. All four wheels could turn round so the only way to steer in a straight line was for one person to run along holding the front end to keep it in a straight line and steer it around corners. This was no good and adaptations were needed. The solution was to fix the front wheels so that they could not rotate but always pointed fore and aft. This was a great improvement and testing recommenced. We were now able to run with two of us behind the bed pushing, and corners were easily rounded by controlling the rear of the bed rather than the front.

The next things to be adapted were the wheels themselves. The small diameter wheels were a handicap on rougher surfaces and did not ride easily over even relatively small potholes. We also believed that larger wheels would run smoother therefore requiring less effort to maintain a high speed relatively speaking. The design for this adaptation was put in place. Pending the change of wheels the two of us continued our test runs and training with the small wheels.

We now had to consider selecting other members for the squad. This proved harder than we had anticipated. Looking back and trying to assess why several thoughts come to mind. Firstly I suppose to someone of sound mind, attempting to break the world bed push record is not a normal every day occurrence. There seemed to be a reluctance to be seen pushing an empty bed about camp. It did not worry me but we are all different. Secondly, it was going to involve a lot of hard training, running miles every day both with and without the bed. Again there was a reluctance to subject bodies to the pain involved. John and I had passed through this pain problem long before the bed push attempt came on the scene, and probably knowing us put some other people off. Thirdly I suppose many thought that this exercise would come to nothing in the long run, and so it turned out in the end, but I get ahead of myself.

The first disaster was a wheel breaking. Shattering would be a better description. A spare was attached. Again testing and training restarted. Still we suffered reluctance amongst the other people on camp to join the attempt. We were confident that as the project developed and progress was made they would join us however. Then tragedy struck again. Another wheel broke. We could not get another spare. The Engineer had not produced the larger wheels, which were now vital to the success of the venture. We were now left with a broken bed and a manager who was losing interest in the project. While it was going well he liked the "glamour" and the hype. When the difficulties arose his enthusiasm waned. Fit though John and I were, we were not fixers and negotiators. The attempt was off. We never did become world bed push champions.

So what happened to the bed? I really cannot remember. Probably dumped at the back of a hanger or some such place. Our world championship attempt was over. We would have to think of another hair brained scheme to do in the future as our blood was young and needed constant stimulation.

And finally of course it was again safe to walk after dark along the quiet roads around the habitated section of RAF Eastleigh without fear of the dreaded spectre of the mad bed pushers looming out of the night.

# Chapter Fourteen

## Around Camp

### Guard duty

Now it was not all sport, holidays and just the occasional amount of work. There were other things such as guard duty; duty clerk, bus escort and we occasionally had emergency test drills.

The guard duties on camp were serious events. It would usually mean a whole week of these duties. Basically what was involved was that after work and your evening meal you reported to the armoury, collected you rifle and five rounds of ammunition and went to the guard control area with the rest of the guard detail. You slept in tents when off watch. You did two hours on shift walking in pairs around the perimeter of the airfield and around the aeroplanes. There would be several pairs of you out at a time. At the end of your two hours you went back to the tent, had a cuppa then tried to sleep in your four hours off watch.

Despite the fact that we were in Kenya and near the equator, at certain times of the year when on guard duty we wore our full UK uniform including our great coats to keep warm as it got quite cold out on the exposed airfield.

It was not exciting especially as you had to report for duty the next day in the office. At times however it got a little worrying. In the middle of the night walking around in the complete darkness, with the only sounds being what you imagined to be wild animals, the occasional drum beating, and shrieks caused by you knew not what, it got a bit jittery. Now we carried five live rounds but they were supposed to be in the magazine and there was not supposed to be one up the spout ready to fire at short notice as soon as the safety catch was taken off. As you will imagine on certain nights a bullet found its way magically into the breech of your rifle. You had to be very careful when going back to the tent that you had removed it or else you were in deep trouble. I always said that we were not out there to stop anything happening by doing anything, except perhaps cry out as we were shot, but rather, they would know something was wrong if one of us did not get back to the tent on time for a cup of tea. Presumably they would then turn out the rest of the guard or call a general alarm. Not a comforting thought that is it. Still as long as it was not an officer in trouble it was all right with the powers that be.

On one occasion I remember one man did fire a round off. It was an accident, but he had to do it while I was on my supposed sleep period. All hell broke lose. Everybody rushing around. Even when he explained it was an accident and that we were not under attack or anything, it took quite a while for things to calm down. Not much sleep that night.

## Emergency Drills

There were two other occasions when rifles and ammunition were issued. The first I remember was a test drill. Fair enough the system should be tested you had to agree. The plan was that if the alarm went off you rushed to the armoury, handed in your ID card, I seem to remember it was called a 1250, in exchange for a rifle and five rounds of ammo, then went to your allotted guard point. Two problems arose on this occasion. Firstly yours truly was not carrying my ID card, something to be fair you were supposed to carry at all times. They would not issue me with a rifle therefore I had to run back to my billet, find my ID card, run back to the armoury, collect rifle, ammunition and then run to my security point. I got a rocket as you can imagine for that episode. That was not all though, many airmen forgot where they were to assemble after collecting their rifles. I suppose that is what test runs are for, but it was just as well it was a test.

The other time could have been more serious. The rugby team had just assembled at the transport depot to go to an away match. We were all on the bus when a call came through to divert us to the armoury. We arrived, were issued with rifles and the usual five rounds of ammunition and driven around to the main gate where we were lined up inside the gate fully armed. There was a little demonstration outside the gate about something which we were never told about. There was a bit of chanting and shouting from the locals. We were there to deter them supposedly. A good question would be whether we would have fired if told to. Technically we would have had no choice, but one of the crowd could have been our billets dhobi boy who was a friend, we just did not know. Anyway nothing came of it but it always struck me that the higher ups could not handle pressure without over reacting.

Regarding the above with hindsight, which is a marvellous gift of course if you have it before the event, it would have dispersed the crowd quicker if they had got the rugby team, unarmed, to go outside and “reason” with the crowd.

## Bus Guard Duty

Our bus guard duty seemed a bind but I suppose was worth while. Each one of us on duty that week would board a bus every morning, armed with a pick axe handle, to travel with the African driver to collect the children of RAF personnel living off camp and bring them in to the camp school. The drivers knew the routes and the children and we were just guards. If there had been a serious kidnap attempt we would obviously have been overwhelmed but there were no problems like that in Kenya then. The only danger I suppose was from a lone villain which you can get in any country and we would have been well able to take care of him.

The biggest danger were the children. Most, as you would expect, were fine, but the odd one would always be a problem. You have to remember we were all young, single and in my case inexperienced in handling young children, as I had no younger brothers or sisters only nephews who did not live with us. After a few days if you showed any sign of being nice they would play you up something terrible and there was nothing you could do to discipline them. You could hardly hit them with your pick axe handle, could you? even if sometimes it seemed like a good idea. I found the best method was to be surly and grumpy from the beginning of the week then they expected no better and left you alone.

I remember that what taught me the lesson on my first week of bus duty was one very young innocent looking little girl. You would swear butter would not melt in her mouth. All innocent smiles the first day and even gave me a sweet. Unwisely I smiled and took it. Day two she talked a little to me. By the end of the week she was a raving dervish in the bus. A lesson learnt the hard way.

Some of the wives were likely to get you into more trouble than the children though, but that is another story and one that should not be told. Not by me anyway as I was either too innocent or slow.

## Head Nearly Cut Off

I mentioned earlier that I nearly had my head cut off once in Kenya. It happened when going out for a ride in a friend's car. He was Scots and owned a two-seater sports car with a "dickey" seat in the back. I think it was a MG, but cars never were, and are still not a passion with me so I could be wrong. They are a necessary evil in my view. Still back to the story. It was my turn in the back and of course I was higher than the others who sat in the low bucket seats in the front. As we drove along Jock suddenly braked and shouted "Get down". We stopped in time but across the road was stretched a strong thin rope tied very securely and at just the right height to clear our low windscreen but not to clear me perched high in the back. We never understood why it had been put there, as most vehicles would have been caught by it and simply broken it with probably no damage caused. It could only have done real damage to a vehicle such as ours and they were rare. I am also sure it was not meant for us as we were hardly on anyone's hit list.

## V Bombers

Talking about the civilian airfield earlier when on the flood relief mission reminds me of the time I was on guard duty guarding one of our V bombers on that civilian airfield. It was the one with the swept back solid type wing, the Valiant I think it was. The runway on our camp was not long enough seemingly for the V bombers to land and take off from. Seemed long enough to me but I was only pay accounts so who was I to argue with the flyboys. This meant however that the V bombers had to land at the civil airport. Now the story put out by our government was that we had V bombers always in flight all around the clock armed with nuclear weapons as a deterrent to any country that would attack the UK. Fair enough if you believed that we had the right to drop nuclear bombs on civilians. I did not agree but as I said before as a SAC (Senior AircraftMan) in pay accounts I was not at the top of the decision making tree in these matters. Anyway I was one of a party guarding this V bomber one-day and one night. Now while on guard on our own airfield we carried rifles with five live rounds as I said earlier. On the civilian airfield this was not allowed. So there we were guarding a V bomber, supposedly carrying a nuclear bomb, and only armed with pickaxe handles. Now in my book they were either kidding that this V bomber carried nuclear weapons or somebody was pretty laid back on security. Why this one was in Africa remains a mystery to me though.

## The Time I was Shot

Now when I am in bragging mode I like to tell the tale of when I was shot in action. I still have the photograph of me outside the hospital, actually it was my billet, dressed in shorts, long socks, shoes, steel helmet, where I got that from I just cannot remember, and all bandaged up around my shoulders and across my chest. The tale after a few pints goes along the lines that at the dead of night our camp was attacked by an unknown enemy who intended to steal one of our more secret aeroplanes. After a prolonged gunfight we drove them off with both sides suffering casualties. I was shot in the chest, but it was a simple flesh wound to the heart and I was soon up and about again.

The truth of course is slightly less glamorous. I broke my collarbone playing rugby, and not even in a proper game but a practice match on camp just before the season started. Missed half a season because of that and had to run the line instead. They also made me treasurer for the team that season which meant I had to make a collection from all the players at the end of each game to build up a fund for the end of season party. Collecting money from rugby players was harder than playing the game I can tell you. It was also a good excuse for me to go away with the team on away trips some of which were great, even if the transport was sometimes a three-ton lorry. Later in the season I got a septic leg after a cut and so most of that season was a dead loss for me.

## Some billet friends

We lived about twenty to a room. Not exactly private. Over the two years in Kenya friends came and went as they were posted in or out, while others you just seemed to drift away from or grew closer to. Looking at photographs I recall some names and faces but am sure I will miss many. Bill Shaw was a Geordie who after a while wanted to go back home to his long-term girlfriend. I wonder if they ever got married. I can remember discussing with Bill him swallowing a piece of foil, complaining of stomach pains and hoping the x-ray would show up as an ulcer. He never did try it though as a medic assured him that they would know, as it was likely to be in a different place when a second x-ray was taken. Bill did get evacuated back home in health grounds though.

Malcolm was another friend. He was from Bradford I think. Liked his cigarettes did Malcolm and not much into running. If I remember correctly the thought of going for a run was sufficient for Malcolm to go and have a lie down. Sorry Malcolm. Malcolm came on many of our game park trips and was on the epic one where we were thrown out of the game park by the rangers.

Spike, I don't think even his mother knew his real name, was from London. Another "thrown out of the game park" criminal. Always had something to say did Spike and almost always cheerful.

Max I have talked about before as my companion on the Victoria Falls trip, he of course was thrown out of the park with us. Did not live in our billet as he was a corporal but was usually around with us when things were happening.

John, nick name Studs, was a long time friend. He was on most trips and was my companion on my Christmas day off camp trip and on the longer holiday in Uganda. John was an ex boy entrant and was in for a long time and was game for most things. He was the other half of the bed push world record attempt with me so you can see he was not idle or retiring. Good friend.

Of course living twenty plus to a room is not always fun. I note in my diary that after a party which I had not attended due to lack of funds "some blokes after a demob party fighting in billet afterwards. Too drunk to make it a good fight but still interesting and entertaining". "Next days entry "found quite a lot of blood on floor this morning from fight last night. Quiet day today". You had to be laid back about things like that.

# Chapter Fifteen

## Sport - Hockey and Athletics

### Hockey

Where I came from hockey was a girl's game. You have to remember not only where I came from, the Rhondda Valley, but also the time that I was living in then. Hockey is now accepted, as a game played by men as well as women, but not then.

Overseas in the forces though you were in a different world. You tried everything if you were at all adventurous and not just a stick in the mud. So I tried hockey. Now if I wished to boast, and why not, I can claim that I played hockey for Wales while in east Africa. If I wanted to be a little more honest I suppose I should admit that I played hockey for the Wales contingent in RAF East Africa. That does not sound as impressive though so let's go back to me playing hockey for Wales. No caps were issued probably because the team was self-selected just for a knock about, or whatever you call a game of hockey, against another makeshift team.

I also played for Admin. Wing against the other Wings and a few local teams. There was no league just ad hoc matches, at least at the level I played in. The pitches were very good as they were dirt, and very flat. Our hardest games were against Asian teams, as they really knew how to play. With them it was not just enthusiasm, there was also skill. That was a factor missing in most of our team. When the chips are down, fitness and enthusiasm take you a long way but if the other team is much more skillful you are on a hiding to nothing. I generally played in defence which I found easier as the ball was generally coming towards you and not from behind or the side as it did if you were in attack. Our goalkeeper was a masochist. His main way of stopping the ball was to use his body, use of pads and stick were secondary in his mind. It worked very well though to be fair. And yes it was Studs, except when I played for Wales, the man who did many trips with me outside camp and was also nearly world bed push champion.

I suppose my style of play could kindly be described as enthusiastic and robust. Well it had to be didn't it, as I certainly was not skillful. I still wonder why they insist on using the wrong side of the stick half of the time. Seems masochistic to me. They kept telling me that body checking was not allowed but as my favourite game was rugby you can see the difficulty I had if being rounded by a skillful player. The penalties given away were often not as damaging as some of the knocks you took from the really skillful players however. Once they had you sussed out, they could cause you quite a lot of pain with their sticks. Not legally of course, but none the less effective, and you had to admire their skill in doing it without giving away a foul. While it might not have been within the rules, I think it was fair when you considered my style of play.

Despite all I have said above I did enjoy my games of hockey even if I did only reach the stage of one step up from completely hopeless. Remember I have a (very) unofficial Welsh Hockey Cap.

## Athletics

Athletics as such was not organised in the RAF in Kenya. There was an athletics track there but it was not well maintained. Athletics for me in Kenya meant road running. I did not enter any competitions, and I do not think there were any there other than the cancelled coastal relay race I spoke about earlier. I have always enjoyed running and in the warmth of Kenya it was a joy. It also passed the time, as if you did not get involved in things like that the time could drag. Anyway our time was to be used not wasted lying around in our barracks. The inner perimeter road around the camp was about two miles long and undulated. None of the hills were steep really. I found it relaxing just running around this circuit four or five times in the evening or on a weekend.

Now there were not that many men there who did such things so very few were better than I was. I recall one who was however. He was more of a naturally gifted runner than I was. He was not with us long though. On one occasion we had gone out for a run and on the last lap around the camp of our four or five he decided that to finish it as a hard session he would run twice around this small roundabout in front of the hospital, while I would not. This lead I would then acquire of about forty yards at the pace we had been running would make us both work hard over the last mile in order to see who could finish first. As soon as we separated I took off as fast as I could short of actually sprinting. Across the flat section, no sound from behind of his approach. Up the hill, still no sound of pursuit. Round the corner, across another flat section, still I was on my own. Round a bend and then along the last straight section. I glance behind and see him closing swiftly. I keep going but he is gaining. Now brains takes over from brawn. At the next hangar I throw up my arms and stop claiming victory. He was going for the next hangar as the finishing line, which I probably would have done as well, if he had not been so close. So we called it a tie. A victory of brain over brawn even if I only got a draw.

It was a great pity that we did not have a RAF athletics team in a local Kenyan league, as I would have enjoyed that. A missed opportunity for me really. Later in life I did compete in the Welsh league although only as a scrubber, competing to gain league points for my club team.

# Chapter Sixteen

## Mombasa

Mombasa is a town on the coast of Kenya. It was the main place where RAF service men went on holiday down at the coast. There were other prettier towns possibly, but Mombasa was the main place. This was because there were more things you could do in Mombasa than in the other coastal towns. I went there several times for holidays and enjoyed them all.

The main method of travel for us down to the coast was by train. It was not a quick journey but a comfortable one. The trains then were the ones with the corridor down the length of the carriage with compartments seating about eight leading off the corridor. I recall one incident on one of the journeys down to Mombasa. Two of us were in this carriage with just a minister for company. We got on well with him, as he was an interesting man. Eventually to pass the time my friend and I played chess. We had a small pocket travelling chessboard. We were fairly evenly matched so games were not over quickly. After quite a while, I am not sure how long but probably over an hour, the game had got quite involved with pieces mainly moved from their original squares and several pieces having been removed from the board altogether. Then disaster. We tipped up the board and all the pieces including the ones removed from the board fell to the floor. I still remember two things that then happened. Firstly, all I said was "Damn". Secondly, we put all the pieces back where they had been before the spill and carried on with the game. Both, I am sure, surprised our minister friend. He was only surprised by the second point I suppose as he did not play chess well, only having just started to play. Experienced players would see no problem in resetting the board. Still I suppose that although we got on well with him, he might not have been fun to be with going around the bars in Mombasa in the evenings.

Mombasa town was a mixture of old and new which is what most towns are. The old was fascinating and exciting. White walled, narrow streets some filled with markets selling everything. The newer part had fewer attractions for us apart from the bars. The beaches were amazing. White sand, palm tree fringed and blue clear water. There was also an old harbour, which was busy in its own way. We always enjoyed our holidays there.

Generally we stayed at a hotel which gave discounted rates for service personnel. After months on camp, especially during the second year when our food had deteriorated, staying at the Moorings Hotel was a dream. It was a small hotel and would be called a Motel now I suppose, as it was really a series of chalets attached to each other. They were white walled with a thatched roof which extended over the walls by quite a way giving a shady porch to each room. The whole hotel complex was built amongst the trees giving a wonderfully cool shady atmosphere. Remember we were now at sea level and it was much hotter than in Nairobi, which was 5,000 feet above sea level. The trees had been taken away from in front of the hotel and the lawns led down to the water. There was a clear view overlooking the sea from right in front of the hotel. The thatched roof was interesting especially at night. You would lie there just before going to sleep and hear constant rustlings in the thatch. It was home to lizards and other crawling type creatures which were not poisonous we were assured so we slept soundly.

I said they gave discounted holidays to service personnel. For whatever reason I do not know, presumably to attract trade, but it certainly did not lower the standard of what I thought was a very nice, comfortable and respectable hotel. The atmosphere of the hotel always made me feel I had to be on my best behaviour, but I never felt that was wrong, it some how felt right. The meals were great. Marvellous choice, well prepared and presented, and plenty of it. Tea was not to be missed. As many fancy cakes and sandwiches as you could eat. Non service people stayed there as well but their appetites were not as good as ours were so we always had plenty in quantity as well as quality. Our time in the hotel was certainly a major part of our holiday although it was not what we went to Mombasa for.

The newer part of the town had a dual carriageway running through it, so it was no hick town. We were not there for the shopping apart from the markets though. The dominating feature of the main street was the tusk arch. Looking at my photos it is hard to judge the height but it must have been sixty feet at least, and the two arches spanned both carriageways. The traffic was light but I see they had quite a large roundabout there, although I cannot remember it. If any oilman is reading, they certainly sold the petrol whose sign is a star. I won't mention the name: why should they get a free advert from me?

There was an old fort in the town, Fort Jesus. I suppose it was a classic fort of that area. It had large arches and high thick walls with walkways around the inside of the outer wall for the defenders to stand on. It was old but in quite good condition. I wonder if the fort was built by the locals to defend themselves from invaders, or as in my country built by the invaders to surpress the local population? Similarly the old harbour in Mombasa was no modern day port, although there was a constant movement of smaller vessels. Many were of course powered vessels but there were many dhows sailing there as well.

In the old quarter there were beautiful mosques, gleaming white and standing out like beacons in the narrow streets. Vasco De Gama Street in my photographs looks quite busy, there I can see several Morris Minors, and a Ford Popular. I also have a photograph of a Medicine Man, which was taken from the back of a moving car, we did not risk stopping to take the photo.

I must have liked Mombasa as I see from my photographs that I was there in October 1960 and also in December 1960 and I also went there in 1961. Nyali beach seemed to have been the favourite beach we went to. The sand was amazingly white. It looked more like salt than sand. All along the edge of the beach were the palm trees and bush. The sea as I said earlier was a lovely blue and always seemed calm when I was there. Now I have never been a strong swimmer, I actually learned while in Kenya at the age of twenty-one. Even I liked swimming in the sea at Nyali as it got deeper very gradually which gives poor swimmers more confidence. The beach went on for miles, a white swath bounded by the green trees on one side and the blue of the sea on the other while topped by the bright blue sky. Real picture postcard stuff.

Judging by my photos I must have had a thing about climbing palm trees, I am climbing them in several photos. As I recall there was one palm tree there which grew horizontally at first then went upwards at a not very steep angle. That was the one to climb, as with clever camera angles you could look very impressive.

In one of my photos I am standing on the pavement in the town smartly but casually dressed and must have been in the sun for many days as I am only one shade off black. Another couple of weeks and I could have been selected for the Kenyan athletic squad if I could only have run about twice as fast as I actually could. Now that is something I would really have liked to have done.

One thing you should always be careful of is drinking enough fluids, non-alcoholic fluids that is, because of the heat. On one occasion two of us got very near to being in trouble because of the lack of fluids after being on the beach all day. It was not so much that we felt thirsty, although we did of course, but that we felt weak. When we got back to the hotel we just could not stop drinking water and soft drinks. We learned our lesson that day and never suffered again.

The nightlife was not very sophisticated but neither were we. It mainly comprised bars. The beer, if you can call the local lager, beer, was not good but was the usual east African beer. Strong but terribly gassy. Neither the nightlife or the beer was very impressive but we were in Mombasa for the sun and the sea so we put up with them and you can get used to most things. Having said that my diary records that Bill and I did make several friends in the local pubs while there.

I remember on one of our visits to Mombasa I was recovering from breaking my collarbone playing rugby. The treatment was to tie your shoulders back with a figure of eight bandage looped around under your armpits and crossed on your back. I had nearly reached the time for the strapping to come off. So what to do about swimming? Only one thing for it. Take bandages off; swim with only one arm, or on my back using just my feet. A borrowed pair of flippers helped and indeed so much so that I could go through the water that way quicker than I could before. After drying off and a little sun bathing one of the boys would tie me up again and away we went. Never did me any harm.

I liked Mombasa that much that on one occasion I hitched to Mombasa on day one, about three hundred and twenty miles, with Brian. We stayed the night in the Rainbow Hotel for ten shillings bed and breakfast so I think the name was more colourful than the actual building. Day two was spent on the beach and the night in the bars, while on day three we hitched back to camp.

# Chapter Seventeen

## Rugby

Now coming from south Wales obviously I had played rugby. I was better at rugby than I was at cricket, soccer, squash, hockey and swimming, but let's not get too carried away with how good I was. I was poor, to be kind, at the other sports, but I liked playing rugby. In the school I went to, from the age of eleven till GCE "O" level, rugby was not a compulsory sport, for the girls that is! Still for me there was no need for it to be compulsory. I played for the school team and occasionally the area team. After leaving school, work and girls took up my time more than rugby did although I still enjoyed watching the sport.

A few weeks after my arrival in Kenya I went to watch the combined RAF and Army camp team playing a local team. They were from the local Army hospital. Now where I came from the spectators joined in the spirit of the game by shouting encouragement, and often other things, at the players and of course the referee. It was accepted then that the spectators would not cast doubt on the parentage of the referee, but casting doubt about whether he should carry a white stick or be preceded by a guide dog was fair comment.

I remember clearly watching my first game in Kenya, sitting at the back of the "stand". In reality just a few planks of wood supported by scaffolding. The game was not very inspirational. My comment enquiring whether the RAF team was playing the staff or the patients from the hospital seemed to me to be perfectly reasonable and to the point. I still had an unmistakable south Wales accent and in certain quarters they assume all Welshmen are great rugby players. Well of course most are superb rugby players, but not all of us. An officer sitting in the front row on hearing my remark turned around, looked at me and asked my name and section. I gave them to him and could not think what I could get charged with, as my comments had not been that serious unless one of the players was a relative of his. I thought no more about it

Two days later I hear my name being read out over the camp tannoy as being selected to play rugby for the station at scrum half. It turned out this officer was an ex player who had been a scrum half in his time. I had not been asked, just selected, not on the basis of anyone having seen me play but on the strength of my comments at the match a few days previously. Now while I was reasonably fit I certainly was not match fit, and neither was I acclimatised to the altitude, remember we were at an altitude of over 5,000 feet above sea level. I went along to the practice session the next night to explain that I needed time to train before playing at that altitude but I joined in the training. I remember it clearly now. A few warming up stretching exercises went all right. Next we split into pairs. First my partner carried me the width of the pitch at a jog. We then switched over and I jogged back with him on my back. End of training session for me. I could not breathe. It left them in no doubt that I could not play for them that week at least. It took several weeks of steady training before I was able to play.

Previously I did mention a little tongue in cheek that I had been awarded a cap for playing hockey for Wales. Well I suppose I could now claim to have a Welsh rugby cap as well. What's a big lie amongst friends? I did after all once play for the RAF Welsh contingent, East Africa. Funnily enough I cannot remember the score but we must have won, what else would you expect me to say?

I was supposed to play on the wing but you just did not get enough of the ball out there to make the game interesting as then one of the wings main duties was to throw the ball into the lineout. Now while accuracy of throw might be important, you certainly cannot call it an exciting duty. These were pre lifting in the lineout days and before the hooker took over the duty of throwing in. To see more action I converted myself to wing forward, as it was called then, not flanker as now. In those days the wing forward was not as big as they are today. The main assets a wing forward needed then were speed, stamina and a liking of tackling. Stamina had always been my asset, I was reasonably fast and tackling can be fun if you do it right. As I only weighed twelve stone fully clothed and soaking wet, and stood only five foot seven inches tall, you will appreciate I was not that interested in the lineout aspect of the game. The line out as far as I was concerned was a chance to have a rest and eye up the opposing outside half and centre to assess damage potential opportunities.

The scrum again was an aspect of play in which an open side wing forward did not put a great deal of effort into unless your scrum was being pushed backwards. Your duty was to get away from the scrum to carry out your harassing work as early as the referee would let you get away with. Good open side wing forwards are born offside.

There were some crafty wing forwards about though. I clearly remember an older one that I played against who not only knew all the tricks of spoiling his opponent, but also had probably invented some of them. At a scrum he would innocently stand up turning his back to you holding his hands out apparently in surprise. It could catch you off balance and slow you down. Round one to him. Next would be the shirt tug as you went past. Again you were slowed down and if you spun round and retaliated it was you of course the ref. would see. Round two to him. Next came the standing away giving plenty of room to run between him and the scrum towards his outside half, with of course the trip carefully applied. Another round to him. Time to make your presence felt. Next scrum he steps aside to let me through again and puts out the foot for the trip. Unfortunately and completely accidentally my studded boot happened to land half way up his shin and travelled down to his instep. These accidents will happen. Didn't have as many obstruction problems after that.

When I see the modern players having drinks during a game I have to smile. I do not begrudge them the drinks and indeed when I am training down the gym now I am constantly taking small drinks of water myself. In my days of course the most you got was a quarter of an orange to suck the juice out of at half time. This brings back to me the occasion of us playing a school in Kenya. They were all young men, as big as us and mostly fitter than the majority of our team, but possibly not so battle hardened. Now with my size I was not a really terrifying sight. With our not having drinks during the game however it did mean that at an altitude of over five thousand feet your mouth got very dry. It meant licking your lips and drawing your lips back exposing your teeth frequently to get some moisture in your mouth. I could see the strange looks my opposing wing forward kept giving me. I probably appeared to be snarling at him all the time. Anyway I did not have much trouble with him that match as I recall.

Of the two rugby seasons I spent in Kenya I really only played for one of them, the second being almost a complete wipe out through injuries. I managed to break my collarbone in a pre season training game, while later I broke my little finger and get a septic knee. The knee was a nuisance as it stopped me running as well for a short while. The broken finger was not a problem as it was easily strapped to the next finger, but these injuries reduced the games I played in Kenya considerably. For that season I was the Treasurer of the rugby team as I was not able to do much else other than run the line. While there were no special financial rules I did manage to collect enough money from the players at the end of each game to pay for a few drinks at the end of the season celebration. It meant I went on all the away trips as well of course.

A final thought on rugby, always remember that rugby should not to be treated as an extremely serious game, it is much more than that, in Wales, it is a second religion.

# Chapter Eighteen

## Local Pleasure Trips

I use the term "local pleasure trips" to mean local in a Nairobi in Kenya context. That is trips of probably up to sixty or seventy miles from base, although the last one was one hundred miles each way.

### Carr Hartleys Animal Park and Hospital

Carr Hartleys was a place out in the countryside in Kenya where the Hartleys had set up what I suppose you would call an animal hospital and recuperation centre. A visit to Carr Hartleys was a joy. You saw wild animals very close up, animals, which were used to human contact. Most of the animals were orphaned or sick baby animals when the Hartleys received them. They were nursed to good health and were mainly hand reared, which is why they were so relatively tame. Most of them that is, although there was one fully grown rhino there which you were told to keep very well clear of as it had a bad temper. Rhino's are not to be tampered with especially if they have a bad temper, a landrover would come off second best in a serious argument with a rhino.

For us based at RAF Eastleigh it was a day trip by car. At this time one of our billet had purchased an old Rover 90. Bruce I think his name was, he stood well over six feet tall and was still a national service man. He was older than most national service men were as he had had a deferment to finish his studies I seem to recall. Anyway it was a steady strong old car. So one day four of us set out to visit the Carr Hartley establishment.

Now while as I said the animals were tame some of them were very large. They were not behind bars or ditches but were completely free to roam as they pleased. To stand leaning nonchalantly against an elephant much taller than you is an experience. The same with a fully grown rhino. After leaning on these two, a picture taken with an eland seemed tame but they are quite large and have mean horns. To run your hand over the back of a baby elephant and give it a cuddle is something else. These things now might not seem so rare but back in the 1960's they were something else.

I wanted one photograph I remember of me standing between a fully grown elephant and a fully grown rhino with my hands on their trunk and head respectively. I thought it had been taken and started to walk back to Malcolm my friend who was the photographer. It turned out he had not taken the shot but took one as I walked towards him and it comes out as if these two wild animals are meekly following me like household pets.

While these animals were by no means wild in the normally accepted sense, you saw them in a wild context, completely free to roam. They could put up with your attention or not as they saw fit.

## Hells Gate

Hells Gate was another local trip but of a completely different type. No sanitised or developed area this. Again it was a visit by four of us from camp. This time we hired a VW minibus for the trip. It did not start off very successfully since immediately after leaving camp we were involved in a road accident, which damaged our vehicle slightly, but not enough to stop us completing the journey before returning the vehicle.

Hells Gate is in the rift valley and was therefore many miles from camp. I seem to recall it took us a few hours to get there and then the hard work began. The minibus to be fair to it took us a good way there off the tarmac road but then our human legs took over after we nearly rolled it over going over ground that was too rough for the vehicle.

The walk was across open ground, mostly dusty with some small shrubs. It was several miles before we reached the entrance to the gorge named Hells Gate. While that walk was enjoyable if you liked that sort of thing, and I particularly did, it was much the same as many walks we had done in other parts of Kenya. Once you entered the gorge however it was completely different. You walked through this dusty gorge with the sides towering above you more as I had seen in cowboy pictures than I had expected to see in Kenya. The cliffs were completely bare of vegetation and the strata and colour of the rocks a sight to see.

At the end of the gorge it climbed steeply and brought you up level with the surrounding ground level. The far end was marked with a cairn and the area there was much greener with quite thick vegetation. After a short stop for a snack and a drink it was time to retrace our steps back to our trusty VW.

The Hells Gate experience was another that many people in the RAF did not have and so they missed a great deal of seeing the real Kenya. I note that Max was one of our party again. Not only did we do the Victoria Falls trip together we did many more by the look of it. He must have liked getting out and about in Kenya as much as I did.

## Thompsons falls

The local language of Kenya was Swahili. It was a reasonably easy language to get the very basics of, although not being a natural linguist I never got further than the basics even though my job was civilian pay. Certainly in the version of Swahili I learned while in Kenya there were some easy ways of expressing yourself, "slow" for example was "pole" pronounced with a long "e". To say "very slowly" you just repeated "pole" twice. "Quick" was "upeci" again pronounced with a long "e". So "very quickly" was "upeci upeci." I think my spelling is right.

I clearly remember in my early days in Kenya trekking through the bush trying to find a well-known waterfall. We had got to the nearest village by hitching and headed off into the bush down trails as we had been instructed by someone who had gone there previously.

After a while we thought that we had gone wrong somewhere so when we came upon some children we put my new linguistic ability to the test. At this point I will explain that the Swahili word for water starts with the same letter as the word for milk. The letter M. Water is "maji, and milk is "maziwa". To these children, this strange man coming out of the bush, asking to be pointed to a lot of falling milk, while making a sweeping motion downwards with his arm, and making a roaring noise with his mouth must have appeared to be someone who should be put in a safe place for everybody's sake. They could not help us which was hardly surprising really, but a short while later we heard the roar of water and found my "milk" falls. For those who have been there it was Thompsons Falls.

Thompsons Falls were quite high by standards other than Victoria Falls. The area around the falls was green and inviting. The falls were most impressive from the foot looking upwards but I suppose most falls are like that.

One other interesting thing of this outing was crossing the equator on foot. I have a photo to prove it. It shows me standing by the equator sign, which proudly proclaims that we are in Kenya at an altitude of 7,747 ft. above sea level. I think that must have been the first occasion I actually walked across the equator, as I cannot see why I had the photograph taken otherwise as we crossed it many times in my two years in Kenya.

Brian Elliot was with me on that trip according to my photographs although there were others as well. Brian was not a great one for venturing out and about and was not in Kenya for long at the same time as I was.

## Thika Falls

I seem to have a thing about waterfalls don't I ?

Thika Falls was only about thirty odd miles from Nairobi and so was a simple trip, which I made several times. The falls were not very high or wide but they were quite pretty and surrounded by very green countryside. We travelled there on different trips by various means, mainly by hitch hiking or by hired vehicle.

The walks to the falls were through the bush, which in a way made it exciting, although I must admit we did not see any wild animals to speak of except monkeys and other small such animals.

For some of us the Thika Falls trip was like a Sunday school outing compared with some of our other adventures but it was enjoyable and a day off camp in different surroundings.

## Christmas Dinner off camp

There was a tradition in the RAF, probably in the other services as well, that the officers serve Christmas dinner to the other ranks. Possibly it still continues today, I do not know. A stupid tradition to me, which reeks of class snobbery and old fashioned thinking from another age long dead. Anyway the only Christmas day I was to spend on camp in my three years was the one when I was in Kenya.

Well this Christmas John, I seem to recall his nickname was "studs" for some reason, perhaps I am wrong, and I were not keen on this tradition, so we decided we would not take part in it. John is the same person who was involved in the world bed push attempt with me, went on many of my day trips, and also was my sole companion on the Uganda trip I will tell you about later. Neither of us was working on Christmas day so after breakfast we left camp and set out for the day. No pack, no supplies, just a few East African Shillings in our pockets.

Our idea was to hitch to Kampala, about one hundred miles away, have a bite to eat then hitch back again. I must admit looking back now I do wonder where we got these ideas from. Anyway off we set and sure enough we got a single lift all the way to Kampala. By now it was lunchtime. So instead of having a full Christmas lunch of turkey with all the trimmings, followed by Christmas pudding, beautifully served no doubt by the officers, we had a meat pie and a bottle of beer if my memory serves me correctly. Quick walk around part of Kampala and back on the road to Nairobi. It was our lucky day as it took us no time to get one lift all the way back again. Remember to be fair there was nowhere between these two places really of any size.

Back on camp we both felt we had enjoyed our Christmas day more than sitting around doing nothing but eat and drink.

As an ex national service man I can see that the tradition of the officers serving the other ranks once a year would strike me as stupid. John however was an ex boy apprentice in the RAF and a long-term regular, so it seems stranger that he thought this way too. He was a friend for a long time, but I have never met or even spoken to him since I left Kenya.

# Chapter Nineteen

## Nairobi and Area

### Nairobi Town

Nairobi to me appeared quite a large town. It had buildings much higher than I was used to back home. Even though we were not rich by what appeared to be the standard of other former Europeans, we did have money to spend and so could afford to go out and enjoy ourselves. One treat we sampled was to sit at the tables outside the New Stanley Hotel in the busy centre of Nairobi and quietly watch the world go by over a few beers or coffee. To us it appeared the place to be.

The tallest building if my memory and photographs are correct was the Norwich Union Building. Perhaps it was the tallest we could get access to the roof of. From the top you had great views of Nairobi stretched out below you. The government buildings were solid, smart and impressive. The main highways wide and the cars modern by the standard of those days and there were many of them.

Anyone in the RAF who stayed in Nairobi I am sure knew of the café whose name I cannot recall which served the best milk shakes in town. There was virtually any flavour you could think of for sale and all tasted rich and full of flavour. To get the best deal the form was that you made sure that you all ordered a different flavour. This meant each was made separately and you were given the glass full, plus what remained in the mixing jug, which amounted to another full glass usually. If two of you ordered the same flavour he could make one jug fill two glasses so you had to be careful. Can anyone remember them? Probably the best drink in town, in the daytime anyway.

Another fascinating sight was the wood carvers. They sat around carving with just a knife and a piece of wood. Mostly they carved the wild animals of the area but they did bowls and such things as well. I still have a set of the three monkeys, hear no evil, see no evil, say no evil; plus a pair of rhino and a pair of antelope heads and a large fruit bowl. Not only did I bring them back with me but also they have moved house with me nine times and are still as good as new. The locally made drums were also a souvenir to keep. I also still have my lion skin and my zebra skin drums in perfect condition. The local markets were a constant interesting way of passing a few hours in town.

Talking of Nairobi Town reminds me of why to this day I cannot drink whisky. I hasten to add that it was not Nairobi's fault but mine entirely. On my first real weekend on camp in Kenya I was going down town on the Saturday night with some new friends from my billet. I had already discovered that I did not like the local beer and so was going to drink shorts. Whisky could be bought cheaply on camp so I acquired a bottle. We were all going to have a few drinks on camp before going down town, as they were cheaper. Unfortunately after a few drinks the whiskey was going down almost like beer, I was a beer drinker not a shorts drinker after all. I can assure you that it catches up with you after a short while. So off to Nairobi we went me with a bottle of whiskey inside me. You will not be surprised to hear that I can recall nothing of that night except waking up the next morning in a RAF cell on camp. I am told I kept slipping off my chair and sliding under the table down town so they put me in a taxi paid the fare and asked him to deliver me back to camp. Nobody came with me. A caring lot they were not. Luckily the Kenyan taxi driver was an honest man and delivered me as asked. The MP's simply put me in a cell till morning, made me clean up the mess and threw me out. Monday morning I was up in front of the Squadron Leader in charge of the accounts department and was given two weeks jankers. He was probably not too impressed with this new recruit to his department. It taught me a lesson though, don't drink the whisky; learn to like the local beer.

## Brackenhurst Hotel

The Brackenhurst Hotel was very pretty. It had very well tended grounds with many flowers and shrubs amongst which you could walk. It was a quiet area and a quiet hotel. It was not the usual place you would expect a party of young men from a RAF camp to visit on a weekend afternoon for tea, but visit it for tea we did. The afternoon tea there was superb. The sandwiches were fresh, thin cut and full of delicious flavoured fillings. The cakes were out of this world as far as we were concerned after RAF food. And best of all you could eat as much as you wanted for the set price. While we ate more than our fair share, I am sure it worked out OK for the hotel, as the more elderly locals did not want as to eat as much as we did.

## Outside the camp

The area directly outside the camp all the way around was out of bounds to service personnel. Nobody explained why but it meant that even if we had wanted to we could not have walked in to town. The choice was catch the bus from the camp gates or get a taxi.

On the way in to town the area was built up with shops and houses for the local people, while around over three-quarters of the perimeter of the camp it was just open bush. The fence was not all that secure in some of the more remote parts of the camp and you could easily get in or out. I went outside through the fence a few times but really there was nothing there to see or do so they were short lived trips.

## Sunset and Sunrise

Nairobi is very near the Equator and so the daylight hours do not vary much from season to season. The fact that the sun always sets about seven in the evening, give or take under half an hour, takes some getting used to at first. While it does mean that you do not get the long light evening at any time of the year, the good thing is that you do not get it going dark at about three thirty in the afternoon either, as you do in the UK in December.

# Chapter Twenty

## Mount Kilimanjaro

Now this trip, unlike most of my visits around Kenya and else where in East Africa, was organised by the RAF. The aim was for us to climb Mount Kilimanjaro, the highest peak in Africa at 19,340 feet.

As the RAF organised the trip it meant that we were provided with transport there and back, accommodation was arranged for us, and we were kited out with all the gear we needed. This was in complete contrast to how we organised our other long expeditions, as you will recall from the Victoria Falls expedition for instance.

The day before we set out we all collected our kit from stores. Waterproof warm jacket, rucksack, woollen hat, woollen gloves, thick underwear, sleeping bag, water bottle and various small items. We were to carry all our own equipment, except food, which would be carried by porters, hired locally at the foot of Mount Kilimanjaro.

We were up very early in the morning as the plan was to drive there and walk up to the first hut on day one. We travelled in a three ton lorry which was effective transport but not exactly comfortable. Although Kilimanjaro is in what is now called Tanzania it was less than two hundred miles from our camp in Kenya. Our lorry took us across the flat section leading up to the start of the climb and we all dismounted and prepared ourselves for the five days walking before us.

So packs on and away we went. The first part of the climb is through semi jungle is the best way I can describe it. The track while well worn was rough and boulder strewn. The trees cut out any views we could have for the first part of the climb. I should state here that climbing Mount Kilimanjaro is nothing like rock climbing at all, but is a long walk with some very serious steep sections.

Before dark we reached the first hut named Bismark. It was of stone construction with a zinc roof and was about nine thousand feet above sea level. It had bunks for us to sleep on in our sleeping bags and generally was quite good considering where we were. Sleep however was hard to achieve. Our main meal was not exactly the highlight of the trip, but then none of them were really. It consisted of a few tins of various meats and vegetables combined with a few dehydrated vegetables and bread boiled in some water to make a kind of thick stew. Unfortunately I was one of the cooks that night. Not good news I can tell you, as I am no cook. As I recall we ate it with relish after our long day, first on the road then walking.

The second day dawned bright and clear. First a very swift wash, then breakfast and away we went on our way up the mountain. Soon we could now see for miles as we were above the tree line. Kilimanjaro has twin peaks. Kibo, which is the snow covered one that is always shown when people talk about Kilimanjaro, and Mwenze, which is a much more rugged and jagged peak. Kibo is the 19,340 foot high peak while Mwenze is the little brother at 2,000 feet less I think. Certainly Mwenze is the lower of the two peaks. They are joined by what is called the "Saddle" for obvious reasons.

All day as we walked we could see at least one of the two peaks, usually Kibo, our final target. The terrain on this the second day was very rough and boulder strewn. It made the walking hard going all day. Of course it was all up hill as well so it was a reasonably hard day but enjoyable none the less. Eventually we reached the second hut and settled down for the night. The meal was about the same, certainly nothing to write home about, but it was warm and I was not helping with the cooking that night, which was a relief for me and probably better for the rest of the gang.

The second hut, named "Peters", was again of stone construction with a zinc roof and the walls were whitewashed and was about twelve thousand feet above sea level. Again considering where we were it was reasonably comfortable. By now it was getting colder but the air was crisp and clear and we could see far into the distance. Until the clouds rolled in that is. Standing there looking up at the peak of Kilimanjaro so clear above you then turning around and looking out across the tops of the clouds was an eyrie experience. It was almost as if we were flying above the clouds. So another night on the mountain. Not such a good night by now for most people. Whether it was the colder atmosphere, which we were not accustomed to, or the altitude I cannot tell. I did not sleep well, however.

Up again early. No problem after not really sleeping. Breakfast, load up and away once again. Very soon on this day we clearly see our goal. Both peaks stand out towering above us. I look at Mwenze and am very glad we are not to climb that one. It looks a very serious climb to me. By comparison Kibo looks gentle and inviting. How wrong can you be! Much of today we are walking across the Saddle and the going underfoot is not so rough. The altitude is starting to affect us I am sure as sometimes I find myself out of breath while just walking. I estimate we were then at about 15,000 feet above sea level. By now we are strung out in a long line over many hundreds of yards. There is no chance of anyone getting lost as the route is quite clear and we can see the mountain peak ahead of us and eventually the third hut where we will grab a few hours sleep. By now I am wrapped up in full gear to keep out the cold and it is still daytime. The pack feels heavier than it did in previous days but we walk on. Even the porters are well wrapped up as protection from the cold. I do not know if we were there at a particularly cold time or whether it is always cold there at that height, but cold it was.

Eventually we reach the third hut. Kibo. This hut was not as comfortable as the others. I clearly remember now that while there were bunk beds there, enough for all of us, there were many slats making up the base of each bed missing. They had probably been used for firewood. It meant that even through our sleeping bags we could feel the gaps, while the edges of the boards that were there cut into us. After supper we tried to sleep but I certainly got very little as I think did most of the group. It was by now also very cold. Despite sleeping in most of our clothes we were all cold. Now to be fair it did not get anywhere near cold enough for anyone to get frostbite, but we were all used to heat and not this creeping cold which seemed to penetrate your bones.

Another problem was socks. Rather the problem was whether to change them or not. Some said fresh socks were best, others that it was best not to change them. I changed mine after three days, got terrible blisters and therefore wished that I hadn't changed them. Painful to walk. Can't win them all.

The target was to get to the top of the mountain before sunrise and we had several thousand feet of loose screed to climb first, so it was a wake up call at 2 o' clock in the morning for us, only a few hours after we tried to go to sleep. A cold bite to eat, a cup of tea and off we set. By now we were into the serious hard walking bit. It seemed to be loose screed all the way. Nowhere could you get a guaranteed safe footing. Your feet constantly slid backwards or sideways. Breathing became harder, and as we zig zagged up the screed we often had to stop to get our breath. It was still bitterly cold and my feet felt frozen. Several times I just fell forward on my face as I think did others. Apparently the altitude was affecting us. Still onward we climbed staggering more than walking in truth until we came to the cave. By now I had a terrific headache and felt sick all the time. The cave I think is about one or two thousand feet from the summit and at that time of the night seemed a warm and inviting place compared with the bleakness of the open mountainside.

It was here that I gave up the climb. I was not alone as several had not got this far, while several more stopped there the same as me. My recollections of the cave and why I stopped are dim. I felt not so much exhausted as ill, weak and sick. Several of us were physically sick, which is not pleasant at the best of times but very unpleasant when you seem almost delirious. At first light those of us who stopped at the cave started walking back down defeated, hoping to feel better as we got lower down the mountain, and so it proved to be the case. We very briefly stopped at the third hut to collect our packs and the rest of our gear and walked on ahead of the others down the mountain.

We stopped at the second hut for the night. The downward journey was so much easier than the upward one. The ease and speed with which we recovered our health and well being was indeed surprising. I am sure by midday of the day on which I had felt so ill in the early hours of the morning I had fully recovered. Except that I had a terrible disappointment inside me that I had failed to beat this mountain, and yet was so fit even at five thousand feet above sea level. The disappointment stays with you for a long time I can assure you.

The section of the party which made it to the summit were full of the praises of the beautiful view of the sunrise. I didn't mind missing seeing the sunrise, but I wanted to get to the top.

Next day we walked down to the base of the mountain, stopped for a short while at a hotel where we met our transport and then drove back to camp. A medic later told me that it certainly was altitude sickness that made us ill but that was not much consolation.

The Kilimanjaro expedition although for me a failure in that I did not reach the summit was a terrific experience, which I would recommend to anyone. Kilimanjaro is a beautiful mountain.

It was a whole week before I could wear shoes again my feet were that badly blistered. I had to get a sick note from the sick bay to wear daps "plimsolls" while I recovered.

# Chapter Twenty One

## Uganda

In July 1960 John, who I mentioned previously as being one of my main travelling companions, and I decided to go to Uganda for a holiday. Uganda was the country next to Kenya towards the west. You will not be surprised to learn that we intended to travel by rule of thumb. That is, we were going to hitch hike there and back, and so it worked out.

We did not have a definite plan of where we would go in Uganda, but Jinja, Kampala and Lake Victoria were our prime objectives. As usual we travelled light just carrying a change of clothes and a little money basically, but of course full of optimism. If a person was only allowed a limited quantity of optimism in their life I am sure I would have used my entire ratio up in my two years in Kenya. It does not work like that though does it.

As usual the weather was fine and warm and of course dry. The Kenyan weather was very dependable. Off we set for Nakuru about one hundred miles north west of Nairobi. We were very lucky and had a lift all the way very quickly. Things were looking good, and in truth they were only going to get better, but we did not know that then, lifts were coming our way easily. And so on to Tororo on the Kenya Uganda border. We had now travelled nearly three hundred miles all in comfortable cars.

The countryside we had been travelling through was basically open bush with the odd village here and there. The roads were mainly straight for long distances and the traffic was very light. During our journey we had crossed the equator and have the photograph to prove it of course. Between Eldoret and Tororo while we were changing lifts I took a photo of a couple of giraffe, standing side by side, heads nearly together like a pair of bookends, staring at us. Not all wild animals live in game parks.

As I have said before most people gave you lifts because they wanted someone different to talk to while driving. On this trip we met several fascinating people who had interesting things to say and were keen in hearing our stories. The people who gave us lifts were always very kind on this trip especially. When we reached a town where they were going to leave us for instance, they would take us to the other side of the town and put us on the right road to continue our journey. Little kindness' like this can save lots of time on your journey, so we were making very good progress.

So by the end of the first day we had reached Jinja and had time to look around. We stayed in a small hotel while seeing the sights. The main attractions seemed to be a Hydro Electric scheme, which seemed fairly large to us at the time, and some beautiful Mosques. Life in Jinja was slow and we did not enliven it I am sure.

Next day and it's off to Kampala only about fifty miles away. One lift took us there the whole way, and what a lift it turned out to be! Now you have to accept that people are not obliged to give you a lift. It is their car and their journey. This lift however was definitely an exception. In the short time we knew the man he not only gave us a lift to Kampala but he then lent us the use of a bungalow for the whole time we were staying there, and that included the use of a dhobi boy to clean and wash. He just drove us to the bungalow, gave us the keys, wished us a good holiday and drove off. No rent to pay, free electricity, what more could you ask for. Looking at the pictures now, forty years later, it still appears to be a modern bungalow. Brick wall, tiled roof, and porch and set in its own garden. For John and I this was real luxury compared with life back on camp. With luck such as this a great holiday was guaranteed.

Kampala is built on seven hills and was quite a large town even then. As it had a Cathedral I suppose it should be called a city, anyway as I enjoyed my holiday there so much that is what I am going to call it. So we now had a base to stay, had got there earlier than we thought we would, and had extra money to spend. Definitely things were looking good.

We walked miles that holiday in Kampala. We were both fit as John was the other main runner in the World Bed Push Attempt. I think we must have made it up all of the seven hills to see the sights. St Johns Cathedral was very impressive in an European style, large, solid, brick building way. The Mosques were equally impressive in a different way. Gleaming white, immaculately clean, with their tall spires and elegant domes. The government buildings were modern and also impressive. Why else would a twenty-one year old in the RAF take a photo of them?

Looking down from one of the hills over Kampala you can see a City of many modern buildings with much greenery amongst the buildings. We lived well that holiday sightseeing, eating well with the odd few beers of course, although neither of us were much in the way of being big drinkers then.

Lake Victoria was a must to visit. It is huge. Approximately a rectangle of one hundred and fifty miles by two hundred miles. It was just like looking out to sea really not like looking at a lake. It is so large that waves break on the shore. While we were there they were small waves it must be said but there was not much wind either to whip them up.

I liked this area so much that the following year I went to Lake Victoria again this time visiting Kisumu which is in Kenya, a trip of only about two hundred miles from Nairobi and we only stayed a few days.

We visited Entebbe, which was not very far away, again by hitch hiking.

Another evening we were invited out to dinner with the Woodleys, we were really pampered this holiday.

Back to Jinja now and we stayed with the Bernards again for a few days while we looked at the sights.

This holiday while not the most spectacular of my trips was the one where we were shown the most kindness on a direct personal level, yet I have no note of the man who lent us the bungalow's name, nor can I remember it.

# Chapter Twenty Two

## Zanzibar

Zanzibar is an island off the coast of Tanzania in East Africa. The island is situated north of Dar es Salaam and south of Mombasa. It is the Spice Island.

It was August 1961 and time for another visit to somewhere I had not been before. Zanzibar sounded good. I had heard it was exotic, warm, and sunny and not many people from camp had been there, if any. Enough reason for a visit in my book. For the life of me I cannot recall who travelled with me but I can remember that there were just two of us. Perhaps whoever it was if they read this will remind me. Probably it was John again. So we booked a travel warrant for a return train ride to Mombasa and away we went. We were allowed some travel warrants free each year as we could not get home for leave presumably, anyway if they were free why waste them?

The first stage by train to Mombasa was uneventful. We then set off to hitch to the nearest port we could find to Zanzibar. Now on this road down on the coast lifts were not so plentiful, so you took one even if was only going a short way relatively. I remember we were stuck at the side of the road on our first day of hitching for a long while when two friendly locals climbed up a tree by the side of the road and got us a fresh coconut each. They chopped the top off and we drank the milk. I am not sure now whether it really is a wonderful drink, or was it that we were very thirsty, but then it tasted like the best drink on earth. They then chopped open the coconuts and we ate the inside. It tastes nothing like the coconut in chocolate bars no matter what they tell you in the adverts. Very fresh bananas were then on the menu care of our new friends. Can affect your stomach if you are not careful though.

Our first stop was Tanga. We stayed there only for a day looking around. Small town but with an impressive town hall.

So onwards to Zanzibar. Lifts improved and anyway it was not very far and soon we were on a boat to our destination. Zanzibar grows cloves as one of its main crops. At least it is the one you smell first, last, and I think always. We first smelt the cloves in the boat while still a fair way off the island. I liked the smell, it was from a different world to what we were used to.

So first job, get booked in to a hotel. Our room had a balcony which judging by the photograph was large. The views from the balcony were picture postcard. White washed walls with red roofed buildings set amongst lush green bushes and palm trees, all under a brilliant blue sky. Why did I not stay there forever? Could not afford it then I suppose, and I would not have wanted to be AWOL again, or I would have had wanted notices out for me like an American cowboy. So a good hotel then. I cannot remember anything of the food so it must have been OK. A good base anyway for the rest of the holiday.

Looking at my photographs I think the hotel must have had a private beach as on all my beach photographs I always note this fact. Anyway nice beach it was. White sand, blue sea, red rocks at one end, and the bush including palm trees reaching down to the edge of the sand. It will not surprise anybody to learn that we spent quite a few days on this beach just lazing around, sunbathing and swimming. As I have said before it was a tough life in the RAF in my days!

But Zanzibar was much more than just a great beach. There were things to see and do.

A rickshaw ride around the town was a must. None of your motorised or pedal powered rickshaws these. Genuine old-fashioned people power pulled them.

There was much to see in the town. I suppose the one place you had to see was the House of Wonders. A three story building with a tall tower in the centre of the front. It was old fashioned but interesting. Apparently it was called the House of Wonders because it was the first building on the island to have a lift in it. Sounds like a good enough reason to me to give it that name. Many of the streets were typically narrow and cool and very shady, but all of a sudden you would come across a brilliant white Mosque towering above you. One splendid Mosque was now a museum.

The ruins of the Old Sultan's Palace seemed more like a ruins from Roman or Greek times with the tall stately pillars still standing. Zanzibar Airport buildings looked more like government buildings from European colonial times rather than an airport, while the dhows in the harbour however reminded you where you actually were.

It was being out in the countryside that I enjoyed best, though. The roads were tarmac, and while slightly narrow, were very adequate for the volume of traffic on them which was made up of bicycles more than motor vehicles. We explored the countryside for a few days. The jungle, which is possibly a harsh word for it, was beautiful and easy to walk through. We visited houses in the bush and watched coconuts and cloves being dried in the sun. A simple but effective process. Those days were good days, but to be fair we never had any bad days in Zanzibar.

Soon however it was time to reverse our journey. This time lifts came almost too easily and we were in Mombasa before we expected. So a few days extra there then on the train back to the hard grind of service life. The Zanzibar trip was another well worth doing and one I am glad I did not miss.

# Chapter Twenty Three

## The Return Home

At last my time in the RAF in Kenya was coming to an end. A sad end I felt, but an inevitable end. There were times on camp when I had been utterly bored and fed up but the good times more than compensated for them, and anyway you forget them. I was due for demob in January 1962 and with the terminal leave due to me should be sent home just before Christmas 1961. My transfer date came through and I went around the camp saying goodbye to my friends and handing back items such as bedding etc. I was to fly home via Aden, which pleased me, as I could have a last look at that place.

So off I flew to Aden. The plan being that it would be just a short stop, then I would be off to the UK. But I was in the RAF remember and things did not just happen like that, not in those days at least they didn't. For some reason there was no room on the next flight, then something else cropped up. Eventually I ended up staying in Aden for two weeks, but I did get home for Christmas. To be fair I did not mind the extra time there, but never qualified for that medal, as again I was not on the permanent staff. I would only have lost it if I had been given one I guess, anyway.

So off I now fly to the UK. It was December. Now I can assure you that December in the UK is a lot colder than December in Kenya, and didn't I know it? I thought my blood would freeze up solid. I arrived at the clearing camp too late to clear that day and had to spend the night there. I was back in the old wooden hut with the old-fashioned coal stove in the middle of the floor again. I went to bed that night in my uniform, covered with all the blankets I could find, plus my greatcoat on top of that. Next day I cleared as it was called and was given a railway warrant to go home. As I was classed as a "Z" reservist I had to keep all my uniform and take it home with me. Some of my things were coming home by sea in a box, which would arrive later.

So off I go in civilian clothes now carrying my kit bags. It was still very cold and I still thought I was going to get frostbite. Two trains and two buses later I arrived back in Gilfach Goch. As I walked home from the bus stop nobody recognised me, partly because not many were about because of the cold, and partly because, while in December they were all very white skinned, I was only one shade off almost black. Remember I had been in Kenya for two years and had topped my tan up in Aden for two weeks.

Actually I was recognised by a large brown mongrel dog that lived in my street and who I had always made a fuss of before my RAF days. His name was Pete. Pete McCann we called him as he lived with the McCann's. Suntan or no he knew me and followed me home. The wife of the family he lived with told the tale for many months of her shouting to her husband that Pete was following a coloured stranger and that she was worried about him.

So I was back home after my period in the RAF. I had gone away for two years national service and ended up coming home just over three years later as a regular.

It was three years I would not have wanted to miss. I hope I have given you a feel of service life in the RAF in the late fifties and early sixties from a different angle, and hope you have enjoyed my reminiscences.

It would be nice to retrace my steps now forty years later, to see how much of what I remember remains and how much has changed. It would be a vastly different experience I am sure, as I could now not be so laid back about my travel arrangements. Still it is an interesting thought. This time it would be without John and those other companions of long long ago.

Conrad Bryant

www.ingramcontent.com/pod-product-compliance
Ingram Content Group UK Ltd.
Pitfield, Milton Keynes, MK11 3LW, UK
UKHW041939190726
13854UKWH00004B/1674

9 781445 253046